Journey Through the Psalms

Scripture References as indicated taken from:

I'm so happy our paths have crossed on this journey through the Psalms. We'll be spending the next nine weeks travelling with the psalmists through the heart of the Bible. The scenery on our trip is pretty unique, because in the Psalms we encounter the words of man to God rather than the words of God to man.

It's okay, you don't need to worry about being led down the wrong path. These words are part of Scripture and fully inspired by the Holy Spirit. You might be wondering why, if the Bible is a book about God, would God's Holy Spirit inspire a collection of songs, prayers, and poetry written by human authors to be sitting right in the middle of God's inspired Word to us?

To answer that we have to go right back to the beginning. Before creation. Before anything existed, except God. He has always existed as God the Father, God the Son, and God the Spirit; Triune God. Through all of eternity He has existed in three parts and has experienced fully the love and joy of relationship within Himself.

So why are we here? How do we fit into all of this? Well, we were created to be in relationship with God. Not out of *need*; remember, God already enjoyed perfect fellowship within the Godhead. He created from a *desire to share* love and the joy of relationship. That's why He made us; to relate to Him. Our chief reason for existing is to glorify God and enjoy Him forever.

That is pretty mind-blowing stuff. When we think that our purpose is to know God, enjoy God, and bring Him glory – well, it's hard not to get excited, and it would make sense that we would want to get to know Him and learn how to relate to Him. This is where the Bible comes in. The Bible is a book (actually a collection of 66 books) that shows us who God is, what He is doing (has done and will do), and how to be in relationship with Him. And in the middle of this collection of books we find the Psalms.

The Psalms are a human response to knowledge of God and in them we see a perfect example of how to relate to God from the place of our human, broken, sinful condition. The psalmists travel the entire range of human experience and emotion: happiness, confidence, delight, and hope. Loneliness, anger, confusion, and despair. And anything else you can imagine.

Life can take our emotions on a roller coaster ride. Our time in the Psalms will teach us how to experience and acknowledge our emotions without allowing them to rule over us. We'll learn to allow our knowledge of God to inform and shape our feelings rather than allow our feelings to shape our image of God. We'll practise the art of communication by praying, and praising, and going deeper into friendship with God.

If you've ever done a road trip before, you know it won't always be pretty. Things get real and that's okay. We don't travel alone as we learn to speak the language of the heart. We can travel with each other, and we do travel together with our perfect Heavenly Father, our brother and Saviour, Jesus Christ, and the indwelling Holy Spirit. That's pretty great company.

Let us continually offer up a sacrifice of praise to God, that is, the fruit of lips that acknowledge his name.
Hebrews 13:15

Arlene Bergen

How We Will Journey Together

Beginning a new journey can be intimidating. Where are we going? How will we get there? What will the road be like as we travel? These are just some of the questions we ask before starting off on a new path. Let me try to help you as best I can with some of them.

<u>Where Are We Going?</u>

Our destination is the presence of God through His Word and through prayer. When we come to God through His Son, Jesus, we are always welcome in His presence. There is no magic formula, no special combination of words, no secret routine we must follow to come before God. But, just like effective conversation between people is grounded in the desire to know each other better through speaking and listening, effective conversation with God is rooted in the desire to know Him better by listening to Him (that's where reading His Word comes in) and then responding (that's the part where we pray).

<u>How Will We Get There?</u>

The most effective path to knowledge of God and relationship with God is regular and consistent time with Him in His Word and through prayer.

There are several levels of study you can choose to commit to before embarking:

1. You can choose to attend/watch the teaching sessions which are available at www.unshakenministries.com.
2. You can choose to attend/watch the teaching sessions and memorize the verses provided for each week of study. (You'll find them in a box in the introduction for each week.)
3. You can choose to attend/watch the teaching sessions and tackle the homework for each week. There is much to be gained from daily and sustained study of God's Word. If you choose this path, no one is going to be looking over your shoulder marking your homework. The commitment is between you and God. If you choose this path and find that some weeks you only complete a day or two of homework, or some weeks you don't write down a single answer but only read through the homework, you are still learning and growing.
4. At the end of each week of homework, you will find either a **Call To Prayer** or a **Digging Deeper** component. The **Call to Prayer,** written by *Deonne McCausland,* is a time of gently coming before our loving Father with the contents of our hearts; a time of building relationship through presence. **Digging Deeper,** written by *Justine Lofgren,* is a time of going deeper into knowledge of our loving Father as He has revealed Himself through specific themes in Scripture; a time of building relationship through revelation. Both of these components build on the homework for the week by taking us deeper into time with God and/or knowledge of God.
5. Any combination of the above.

No one will hold you to your chosen path, however, can I ask that you commit to one before beginning the journey? Prayerfully come to God with the specifics of your heart and your circumstances, asking Him to reveal to you the path that is best for you. Choose your path from the place of freedom you have in Christ, not because of guilt. Our Saviour is gentle with us. But He is also doing His work in us, and growth requires some stretching.

What Will the Road Be Like?

One of the best ways to keep to the path is to travel together. If you are beginning this Bible Study alone, good for you for committing to travel even without companions. However, if you can get a friend or two, or maybe a couple of family members to join you on your journey, you will find the path richer. Travelling companions keep each other accountable and provide encouragement when the way gets hard.

You'll likely do most of the study components on your own - time between you and God that is unique and individual. But if you're part of a group that is holding each other accountable, meeting once a week to discuss the journey before watching the teaching session is recommended. As you get together to discuss the content for the week, time constraints often don't allow us to discuss every question or point that was covered. You'll notice some questions each day that have a ➡ next to them. This indicates that these are good questions to discuss as a group. There are also statements in **bold** throughout the homework which can be additional jumping off points for conversation.

I don't know the specifics of your journey; God has a race laid out for you to run, and your race is unique to you. But we run our races together, as well. Not competing against each other for a single prize, but helping each other along the way. Running in such a way that we all may win the prize for which He has called us heavenward in Christ Jesus.

Table of Contents:

Introduction to the Psalms: Listening Guide

Hearts & Minds: We allow God to shape and inform our feelings rather than allowing our feelings to shape and inform our view of God.

1. Feelings are not always accurate <u>indicators of truth</u>, but they are _____ and they are _____.

Context tells us: Who, What, When, Where, Why, How

2. The Psalms come from the genre of poetry. Poetry uses words to _____ _____which represent a deeper truth or concept.

3. Hebrew poetry was not driven by rhythm or rhyme, but by parallelism. Parallelism is where the opening line makes a statement and the second and/or third lines modify the thought by <u>embellishing it or contrasting it</u>. This means the power of Hebrew poetry is not _____ ____ _____.

4. Many different <u>authors</u> at many different <u>times</u> and in and to many different <u>situations</u>. *What?!* The ambiguity surrounding much of the context of the Psalms is what gives them a sense of _____ _____.

5. The overarching theme uniting the Psalms is <u>Creator God</u> is the _____ _____! The book of Psalms is a collection of five books, each with its own sub-theme, but each book _____ the main theme.

Psalm 1 and 2 are the introduction to the Psalms.

View this teaching session at www.unshakenministries.com

6. **Book One: Psalms 3-41.** The psalms of <u>David</u> dominate this book. Theme: _____ but not _____. There is only One who can save, but He can save!

7. **Book Two: Psalms 42-72.** Once again, <u>David's</u> psalms dominate this book. Dominant theme: _____ and _____; the tone is more <u>urgent</u> than Book One. Book Two ends with the picture of a righteous king: this is what <u>could</u> be.

8. **Book Three: Psalms 73-89.** Book Three is the <u>darkest</u> book of them all; sometimes called the book of _____. Book Three raises serious questions: Does God _____ His _____? What if He doesn't?

9. **Book Four: Psalms 90-106.** It is the _____ _____ of the Psalms and opens with a psalm of <u>Moses</u>. *Why him and why here?* God is saying, "Look back at a time before David when I was your <u>King</u>." Dominant Theme: The _____ _____!

The God of the promises is the King who keeps His promises! That is the <u>truth</u> that refutes the <u>feelings</u> of doubt from Book Three.

10. **Book Five: Psalm 107-145.** Dominant Theme: _____ _____ _____. God will not forget His promises!

Conclusion: Psalm 146-150.
Louder and louder shouts of Hallelujah! Praise Yahweh!

We must learn to measure our feelings and circumstances based on the truth of eternity and the One who holds it in His hands.

View this teaching session at www.unshakenministries.com

Week One: Entrance to The Psalms

a WORD to the wise

We stand on the cusp of a journey. Our time in the Psalms is motivated by our desire to know God better by encountering Him through His Word. Throughout the Scriptures, we see reminders of how important it is to know God's Word so that we can live in greater obedience to it. Psalm 1 tells us to delight in the law of the Lord and to meditate on it day and night. Psalm 37:31 reminds us that when the law of the Lord is in our heart our feet do not slip.

If our desire is for the Word of God to dwell in us richly, what better way for it to take up residence in our hearts and minds, than through memorization? Each week will have a memory verse that relates to the week's theme or lesson.

Spend some time at the start of each day's homework learning the verse so that by the end of the week you have it memorized. As this practice becomes habit for us, may we proclaim with the psalmist, I have hidden Your Word in my heart that I might not sin against You.

Here's our verse for week one...

Blessed is the man who does not walk in the counsel of the wicked

or stand in the way of sinners or sit in the seat of mockers.

But his delight is in the law of the LORD, and on His law he meditates day and night.

PSALM 1:1-2 NIV

Day One: Blessed is the Man . . .(Psalm 1)

I love interior decorating. When I walk into a new space I often play a mental game where I imagine how I would decorate the room if it were mine. I think about the purpose of the space and the tone I would want it to convey, then I arrange the furniture, hang pictures, and add lighting so it best fulfills its purpose. One of my favourite spaces to work with is the entrance. It is here that you set expectation and make that all important first impression.

Psalms 1 and 2 are the entrance to the entire collection of the Psalms. They are placed strategically and intentionally to set the tone and expectation for the rest of the book.

We will be spending the next four days in Psalm 1 and then concluding the week in Psalm 2.

1. Let's begin today by reading Psalm 1. What four words comprise the opening phrase?

2. Use a dictionary to find and write down the definition for the word, 'blessed.'

Having stepped through the doorway of the Psalms, we immediately see that we are being shown the way to deep, lasting, happiness and satisfaction. We are being shown how to find favour with God.

This is worth looking into more deeply . . .

 3. According to Psalm 1, what does a blessed person look like?

4. What do we gain from living a blessed life?

 5. Based on your answer to question 3, what would the opposite of being blessed look like?

One of the best ways to gain a deeper understanding of a key term is to look at where else in the Bible the word is used.

6. How would you define the word blessed based on its context in the following verses:
   a. Romans 4:7-8

   b. 1 Peter 4:14

   c. Matthew 5:3-12

7. How has your understanding of the word 'blessed' broadened by seeing it in these different contexts?

8. How is this understanding different from the world's definition of blessed?

9. James 1:12 begins with the words, "Blessed is the man who . . ." does what? Why does this blessing come? (Hint: find the word 'because,' the reason will follow.)

   a. What will be given to those who have stood the test?

   b. What similarities do you see between this verse and Psalm 1?

We have taken our first step into the Psalms and what we see is that our God, great King of the universe, is showing us how to be favoured by Him. Sinful and rebellious people can feel the smile of heaven. That's happy. Not a run-around-goofy, everything's-going-to-turn-out-just-peachy-here-on-earth, kind of happy. (It might work out that way, but not likely. Sorry. We need to be realistic on our trip together.) No. Instead, it's a deep contentment of the soul, because even when things don't turn out perfectly here, we've got a better hope, kind of happy.

If you were making a list of what made you happy, what would be on it? If God was making a list of what made you happy, what would be on His? Do you trust His list for you?

10. What would it look like to trust God's list for you? What items on that list are you having a hard time trusting?

Sin has broken our hearts, therefore, the desires of our hearts are out of alignment. What we think will make us happy can look very different from what God says will make us happy.

The Psalms are a collection of heart cries. God wants us to pour our hearts out to Him – in their broken state! Please hear that! He does not want you to get your heart in order first so He can accept it. He wants you to bring it to Him so He can heal it. Shape it. Make it new.

Our time in the Psalms will show us how to communicate with God by giving us examples of how other people throughout the centuries have laid out their hearts before Him. God wants to be in relationship with us and being in relationship involves getting to know each other and learning ways to communicate with each other. God communicates with us through His Word. We communicate with God through prayer.

For this reason, our journey through the Psalms will end with daily prompts to prayer. Sometimes we will read a written prayer, more often than not, we'll fashion our own prayers by following some basic prompts and turning to Scripture.

One of my favourite things is starting a new journal. Clean blank pages suggest hope and promise. If you have a journal laying around somewhere, pull it out. We'll use it through the course of this study. If you don't have one, can I suggest you try to get a hold of one? Write down your prayers. Include the Scripture reference(s) your prayer is based on or shaped by, as well as the date. Now you'll have something tangible to go back to time and again as you journey with God.

Talking to God:

Reflect on the knowledge that the Creator of the universe longs to be in relationship with us and to shower His favour and presence on us. Though He could have abandoned us in our sin, He did not and does not. He knows the way of His children.

As we see His love and care, we are moved to confess that many times we would rather find counsel with sinners than delight in God's law. Too often we are passively sprawled out on the sofa of entertainment rather than actively digging into the Word of God. We may need to be honest and admit that our idea of blessing looks different than His.

Ask God to shape your heart's desires so they line up more closely with His. As you close, thank God that though He is high and lifted up, He also dwells with those who are humble and lowly of spirit. (Isaiah 57:15)

The LORD spoke to Moses, saying, "Speak to Aaron and his sons, saying,

Thus you shall bless the people of Israel: you shall say to them,

The LORD bless you and keep you;

the LORD make his face to shine upon you and be gracious to you;

the LORD lift up his countenance upon you and give you peace.

So shall they put my name upon the people of Israel, and I will bless them."

Numbers 6:22-27 ESV

Day Two: Who Does Not . . .(Psalm 1)

Yesterday we saw that there is a way to be blessed. There is a way the righteous walk in. Today, we will be looking at what this way does *not* look like. Modern psychology tells us it is more effective to form instruction and develop expectation from the positive. (For example: I could have written, "modern psychology tells us not to form instruction and develop instruction in a negative way," but I didn't because it wouldn't be as effective.)

For example, if your desired outcome is a tidy entrance, you'd instruct the people using it to please line their shoes up neatly and hang up their coats rather than telling them not to kick off their shoes and throw their coats on the floor.

I am a mother of four. I'll be honest, the first time I may sweetly and kindly inform the people who follow me in from the mini-van to please line up their shoes and hang up their coats so we can all enjoy the beauty of a tidy mudroom. (Hmmm . . . that title itself sets a certain expectation . . .) But, the second and subsequent times, I'm more prone to ask them to stop kicking off their shoes and throwing coats and backpacks around.

While in a University Communications class, I learned that there is an exception to this rule. In a situation where the consequences are dire, warnings must be stated in the negative form. If the situation is serious, you don't waste time with extra words. Negatively worded warnings sound more ominous so they are taken more seriously.

When my children were younger, we loved to walk along a system of irrigation canals and drop-gate structures near our house. The water formed into whirlpools at each gate as it moved through the canals. Because of the whirlpools, each drop-gate structure was fenced off and marked with a large sign that proclaimed in bold red: **Warning! Certain and imminent death will occur if you enter these waters.** The warning was followed by a graphic image of a stick person being sucked under the water into a whirlpool they couldn't escape from.

The danger was real. The sign boldly shouted what not to do and why. It didn't waste time with warm fuzzy language.

Psalm 1 begins with, "Blessed is the man who," but then immediately tells us what the blessed man does NOT do.

1. Read Psalm 1 and make a point-form list of what the blessed, or righteous person does not do. Include any other words of warning in this Psalm.

2. Why do you think the Psalmist starts out with the picture of what the righteous person does not look like?

The Psalms are an example of Wisdom Literature, and one of the characteristics of Wisdom Literature is that it expresses absolute truth in black and white. It does not suggest shades of grey. Proverbs is also part of the genre of Wisdom Literature.

3. Read Proverbs 4:10-27. Make a point form list of all the parallels you see between this passage and Psalm 1 (noting both positives and negatives).

    a. What warnings are given in verses 23-27?

    b. What does verse 22 say these instructions are to the one who keeps them within their heart?

4. In Jeremiah 17:5-8 we see a contrast between two images: a shrub and a tree. Read the passage and fill in the chart below by writing words and descriptions that characterize each. (Put a bookmark in this chapter - you're coming back to it.)

SHRUB	TREE

a. Which picture depicts your spiritual journey right now?

 b. In what ways are you intentionally seeking to be planted by the river, nourished and sustained by God?

5. Read Jeremiah 17:12-13. Based on these two verses, what is the end result of the one who is like the shrub and the one who is like the tree?

The danger of sin is real. The consequences are eternal. This is what led David to pray in Psalm 32, "Blessed is the one whose transgressions are forgiven, whose sins are covered." (Psalm 32:1) In great love, God issues a warning. To heed this warning is to discover deep blessing and lasting satisfaction.

Talking to God:

What have you seen today of the character of God? God could remain hidden and distant. He doesn't. God sees our hearts and knows their true state. Pour out what is sick and in need of healing to Him. He sees it all anyway. Wouldn't you rather uncover it before Him so He can deal with it instead of wasting time trying to keep covered something He already knows?

Ask God for help on your particular path – what keeps tripping you up, leading you onto another path, or distracting your gaze? Thank Him that He has not left you to walk the path alone; He sent His own Son to walk the way of humanity perfectly. He is our companion on the journey.

Therefore let all the faithful pray to you while you may be found

Psalm 32:6 ESV

Day Three: Who Does . . .(Psalm 1)

Yesterday we spent time studying what the righteous man does not do. Today we will look at what they do.

1. Read Psalm 1 again, concentrating on the second verse. What does the righteous or blessed person do? See if you can write down two specific things a righteous person does putting your answer in your own words rather than copying from the Bible. (*ASIDE: Putting something in your own words helps you to understand it more deeply. If you're struggling, maybe it's because there is a word you don't fully understand - look up the definition. Sometimes seeing a passage worded in a way that means the same thing but uses different words is helpful. Maybe reading Psalm 1 in some different translations {ESV, NIV, NKJV, NASB, HCB, for example} would help. A website like www.biblegateway.com is a great resource because it allows you to look up and read a passage in many different versions.*)

Psalm 119 is, by far, the longest of the Psalms. It is 176 verses long, making it the longest chapter in all the Bible – even longer than some entire books of the Bible. Let's find out what this Psalm is all about.

2. To read the whole Psalm would take a while, so read the following verses from 119: 16, 35, 54, 96, 127-131. Based on these verses, what would you say is the theme of Psalm 119?

3. In Psalm 119:68, 89-91, 137, 151, we see some of the reasons the author of Psalm 119 loves the law. (Synonyms used for the word 'law' include: instruction, testimonies, precepts, statutes, commandments, rules, word)
    a. In what ways do you see God's character revealed through His law in the above verses?

    b. Why is it important that we recognize this?

4. To help us understand, let's look at it from the opposite perspective. What if God did not show us how to live our lives, how to be satisfied, how to have His favour? What if God did not reveal His character to us?
    a. Would that change who He is? (Hebrews 1:10-12, Hebrews 13:8, and Revelation 1:8 have something to say about this.)

b. How about us - how would our response to God be affected?

God has always existed. He will always exist. His character is unchanging. If God did not reveal His law to us, He would still be absolutely holy and completely just, but we wouldn't have any idea how to deal with that.

Scary thought isn't it?! Suddenly, God showing us His Law seems pretty wonderful, doesn't it? That's why the authors of Psalm 1 and Psalm 119 were excited about the instruction of God.

Think of something that gets you excited: How much you talk about it or think about it? How often do you try to direct conversation towards it, just so you can talk about it some more? When we really love something, we don't just tolerate it, pay lip service to it, or spend time with it when it's convenient or necessary. We get our delight from it. It's running through our heads night and day. Just the thought of it excites us and we feel like we'd do almost anything to spend more time with the object of our affection.

That's partly why social media is hard to resist. Because it is a way to proclaim to people who or what we love, and a way to see what is driving the affections of others. Our social media profiles are collections and displays of our affections.

What we love changes us. It impacts choices we make and how we live.

5. Read Jeremiah 15:16-17. There are three main parallels between these verses and Psalm 1. What are they?

a. In Jeremiah 15:17, what does he *not* do (two things) and what **does** he do? Why?

 b. How does delight in God's word impact behaviour?

I can think of no other way to close today, then to come to the Gospel. Because the truth is, sometimes it's easier to get excited about a new movie, restaurant, or shopping trip, than the Word of God. It's easier to get wrapped up in family and friends than it is our God who has promised to never leave us or forsake us, but often feels distant. It's easier to sit in the company of others than to sit alone.

The Gospel tells us that we all have disordered hearts. We love the wrong things. Or maybe the right things but in the wrong order. We need the good news that God intervened in our sinful human state while we were dead in it.

And you were dead in the trespasses and sins in which you once walked, following the course of this world . . . among whom we all once lived in the passions of our flesh, carrying out the desires of the body and the mind, and were by nature children of wrath, like the rest of mankind.

But God, being rich in mercy, because of the great love with which he loved us, even when we were dead in our trespasses, made us alive together with Christ – by grace you have been saved.

Ephesians 2:1-5 ESV

Talking to God:

Let's close today by praying the words of Psalm 119:173-176:

Let your hand be ready to help me, for I have chosen your precepts.

I long for your salvation, O LORD, and your law is my delight.

Let my soul live and praise you,

and let your rules help me.

I have gone astray like a lost sheep; seek your servant,

for I do not forget your commandments. ESV

Father, let your hand be ready to help me as I seek you.

Day Four: They are Like . . .(Psalm 1)

In this first week of homework we're moving slowly through the opening two psalms because they set the tone and expectation for the rest of the book. So far, we've covered a lot of ground with Psalm 1. On day one we saw that God wants to show us the way to be blessed – the way to deep, lasting satisfaction and favour with Him. In our second day of homework, we looked at what a righteous, or blessed person, does not do. Yesterday we looked at what they *do* do.

Today we will be looking at two pictures that Psalms 1 paints for us. The psalms are poetry and so they rely on poetic device to convey meaning. Poetry is different than prose. In prose, you use straight forward language to get your idea across. Poetry uses words to paint pictures. Pictures leave us with an image to visualize, think about, and they guide us towards uncovering a deeper concept.

We've read Psalm 1 every day this week in the hope that it will become very familiar to us. That should help us as we move forward today.

1. Read Psalm 1 and then read Psalm 26. How do they compare? Note similarities between the two psalms.

2. What is the verb (action word) in Psalm 26:9, and what is the verb in Psalm 26:12a?

   a. Now compare them to the verbs in Psalm 1:4 and 5.

   b. How do these words visually depict what happens to the blessed versus the wicked?

3. Psalm 1:3 paints a picture of the righteous person. Write down each image that the author uses and what you think the image is supposed to convey.

We're going to look at a verse in Ezekiel chapter 47, but to really understand it, we need to have some context. Ezekiel chapter 47 is part of a vision Ezekiel received from God. The vision begins in Ezekiel chapter 40 and concludes in chapter 48. God is showing Ezekiel the new temple, a future temple, in which God's glory will again dwell.

The first eleven verses of Ezekiel 47 tell us about how Ezekiel is following a guide into the sanctuary of this new temple. There is a river flowing out of the sanctuary and the further they walk into this river, the deeper it gets. There are trees along the banks of this river.

4. With this as your background, read Ezekiel 47:12. What does this verse tell us about these trees?

5. What is the purpose of the trees' fruit? What is the purpose of the leaves?

6. What feeds these trees and where does it come from?

7. Read the words of Jesus in John 4:13-14 and John 7:37-38. How do His words deepen your understanding of this verse?

Do you see more clearly the picture the Psalmist is trying to paint of the righteous?

We learn the basics of survival pretty early. Water, food, shelter. We've got to get them from somewhere. Where are we going for the essential elements of survival?

Where we go to survive influences us. What will we allow to influence us? Will we allow the counsel of the world to shape us? Or will we allow the Word of God to shape us? As we are influenced, we influence others. Will our lives be green and bearing fruit, or will the substance of them be like the chaff that is thrown up to be blown away by the wind because it can't be used for anything?

Ponder: *The righteous one is planted strategically. Are you planted strategically, in a place where there is abundant nourishment?*

We are broken people living in a broken world in need of healing. There is only one true Healer. Planted in streams of living water, we are sustained by the Great Physician. Grounded in Him, we can point the broken people around us to the only true source of healing. Abiding in Him, our lives are marked by consistency; always bearing green leaves. And when the season for fruit is right, through His grace, it will be there.

Then the angel showed me the river of the water of life, bright as crystal,

flowing from the throne of God and of the Lamb through the middle of the street of the city;

also, on either side of the river, the tree of life with its twelve kinds of fruit,

yielding its fruit each month.

The leaves of the tree were for the healing of the nations.

Revelation 22:1-2 ESV

Talking to God:

As you conclude, turn Psalm 1 back to God in prayer.

Adore Him for who you have seen Him to be this week.

Confess who you have seen yourself to be.

Because you have seen both God and yourself more clearly, ask Him to change you. Ask Him to use your circumstances to paint your life portrait to resemble the picture we saw in Psalm 1.

Thank Him that He will do it.

And I am sure of this, that he who began a good work in you will bring it to completion at the day of Jesus Christ.

Philippians 1:6 ESV

Day Five: The Reign of the Lord's Anointed (Psalm 2)

Our final day of homework this week will be spent in Psalm 2. I know. You're probably thinking after spending four days in Psalm 1, how can we do justice to Psalm 2 in only one day? We can't. In part, that is the beauty of the living and active Word of God. There will always be more than we can take in. Rather than let that thought overwhelm us, we can delight in knowing that we drink from a fountain that will never run dry.

One way of summarizing Psalm 1 and 2 is by saying that Psalm 1 is about the one who worships and Psalm 2 is about the One who is worshipped. While simple, it's concise, and can be a helpful way of looking at these two Psalms. That means that today we will be looking more closely at the One who we are meditating on - the One we are to worship, adore, and serve.

Let's get right into Psalm 2. We'll break it up into four sections to help us understand it better.

 1. Read Psalm 2:1-3 carefully. What is the situation? What's going on in the first three verses of Psalm 2?

 2. Now read Psalm 2:4-6. We saw the situation from an earthly perspective in verses 1-3. How does the Lord respond in verses 4-6? What is heaven's perspective?

Before we tackle Question 3, here's a bit of background: In 2 Samuel 7:1-17, God makes a covenant with David. God says that He will take David from caring for sheep in a pasture and make him into the king of His people. God has been with David and He has defeated David's enemies. God tells David He will build his house into a kingdom that will last forever. The steadfast love of Yahweh will not depart from David's descendants like it did from Saul, and the throne of David will be established forever.

The model of the righteous king in Psalm 2, the king that is the Lord's Anointed, is in one sense, King David. The model of a righteous man from Psalm 1 is also a picture of David, the man after God's own heart.

King David is part of the picture. But he is not the whole picture. Luke 24:27 tells us that all of Scripture points to Christ. The Messiah. The Lord's anointed. All the covenants the Lord made with Abraham, with Moses, and with David, are fulfilled perfectly in Jesus Christ. In fact, the words 'Messiah' and 'Christ,' both mean the Anointed.

We'll see that many of the psalms are attributed to David. But we can't forget that if David is where they end, then, while it might be good history, by now, it's mostly irrelevant. David was part of the picture. But he, like those who came before him, was only a foreshadowing. Only the hint of a much fuller picture. A picture that is completed perfectly by Jesus Christ.

3. In Psalm 2:7-9, we hear the Messiah's response. What does He say?

4. Read Psalm 2:10-12. Psalm 2 ends with a word to the wise, a warning. What is it?

5. Read Revelation 6:16-17. What connections do you see between these verses and Psalm 1 and Psalm 2?

 6. Read the last line of Psalm 2 again. What do you think is the significance of ending Psalm 1 and 2, the entrance into the Psalms, with this line?

Talking to God:

Spend time flipping through your homework notes to refresh your understanding of who this God we pray to is.

Search your heart to see more clearly who you are and how you are coming to Him. Lay it all at His feet. There is comfort in the warning. There is an invitation to kiss the Son.

This isn't a sappy emotional Jesus-is-my-boyfriend, invitation. This is a very real invitation that assures us we can come to the Lord's Anointed, the Son, knowing we can take refuge in Him from the anger and wrath we rightly deserve.

That kind of makes you want to end your prayer with some praise, doesn't it?

I can't wait for our group teaching session where we tie all the learning we've been doing this week together!

And it is my prayer that your love may abound more and more, with knowledge and all discernment, so that you may approve what is excellent, and so be pure and blameless for the day of Christ, filled with the fruit of righteousness that comes through Jesus Christ, to the glory and praise of God.

Philippians 1:9-11 ESV

CALL TO PRAYER

When digging into God's Word for the purpose of study, it is helpful to search the Scriptures in a translation (e.g. NIV, NKJV, ESV). Yet, when I am looking to pray Scripture, I also look to some of the paraphrased versions (e.g. MSG) or a 'thought-for-thought' (as opposed to the literal 'word-for-word') version such as the NLT. A paraphrase helps me to understand how to put my own words into my prayer. I find these to be helpful tools in putting context and language together to bring before the Lord. As I consider a passage, reading it in a number of versions enables me to 'chew' on the words and meaning throughout the day as the Lord brings it to mind. I can then pray it throughout the day and have the Lord speak to me through it in an ongoing conversation. I receive great joy as He brings other passages to mind that are consistent with what He is speaking into my heart and mind.

I have heard meditation likened to a cow chewing the cud. Maybe not a pretty picture, but one that has helped me understand what I'm supposed to be doing with Scripture as I focus on it for a length of time. The point is to bring it back up to the forefront of your mind over and over. I read it and chew on it a bit (maybe looking at the same passage in a few different versions), thinking about the words or phrases or concepts that strike me. I partially digest and receive nourishment from the words. As I go about my daily activities (often driving or housework), I ask the Holy Spirit to speak His truths into my mind and heart, and as He brings the Scripture 'back up' into the forefront of my mind, I can chew on it some more. The Lord might bring other Scriptures to mind that closely relate to the original verse/passage and I am able to further digest, again gleaning greater nourishment as this can happen all throughout the day. I find this becomes an easy way to pray continually, having an ongoing conversation and communion with Jesus.

Practice

As we spend time this week studying Psalm 1 and 2, we have asked ourselves whether we are allowing the world's counsel or God's Word to shape us. While God can and does impart wisdom in and through our 'world,' as Christians, we are to take care that we are not looking to the world for answers, but seeking God first and perceiving the voice of current culture in light of Scripture, rather than trying to 'fit' God's Word into the world's message. In Psalm 1, we considered the 'way of the righteous' as well as the 'way of the wicked.' I am reminded of the Sermon on the Mount and the topic of narrow and wide gates in Matthew 7: 13-14. When we feel unsure of the way we should take, rather than being overwhelmed, we can trust in knowing THE WAY (as in the way, the truth and the life). Jesus is always the answer.

Read Galatians 5:16-25
(out loud if possible)
Does anything stand out to you?
Ask the Holy Spirit what He wants to show you.

Read the passage from the Message (paraphrased version) below:

My counsel is this: Live freely, animated and motivated by God's Spirit. Then you won't feed the compulsions of selfishness. For there is a root of sinful self-interest in us that is at odds with a free spirit, just as the free spirit is incompatible with selfishness. These two ways of life are antithetical, so that you cannot live at times one way and at times another way according to how you feel on any given day. Why don't you choose to be led by the Spirit and so escape the erratic compulsions of a law-dominated existence? It is obvious what kind of life develops out of trying to get your own way all the time: repetitive, loveless, cheap sex; a stinking accumulation of mental and emotional garbage; frenzied and joyless grabs for happiness; trinket gods; magic-show religion; paranoid loneliness; cutthroat competition; all-consuming-yet-never-satisfied wants; a brutal temper; an impotence to love or be loved; divided homes and divided lives; small-minded and lopsided pursuits; the vicious habit of depersonalizing everyone into a rival; uncontrolled and uncontrollable addictions; ugly parodies of community. I could go on. This isn't the first time I have warned you, you know. If you use your freedom this way, you will not inherit God's kingdom. But what happens when we live God's way? He brings gifts into our lives, much the same way that fruit appears in an orchard - things like affection for others, exuberance about life, serenity. We develop a willingness to stick with things, a sense of compassion in the heart, and a conviction that permeates things and people. We find ourselves involved in loyal commitments, not needing to force our way in life, able to marshal and direct our energies wisely... Since this is the kind of life we have chosen, the life of the Spirit, let us make sure that we do not just hold it as an idea in our heads or a sentiment in our hearts, but work out its implications in every detail of our lives.

What words seem to repeat?
How do you relate this passage to our study of Psalm 1?
What is the Holy Spirit saying to you? (Understand that as you ask Him, and wait for His answer and leading in your heart, you are entering prayer - communion with God through Christ our Royal Priest and by the Holy Spirit.)

On Our Knees

In a spirit that is open to God's light being shone to expose any darkness, pray Psalm 139:23 and Psalm 26:2, then pray that God would align your thoughts with His (even if this takes days of praying).

If it is hard to submit a particular way/pattern of thought or perception that lines up more closely with the world's view than with God's view (be aware that His view is most likely going to be different than the world's view for the world's ways are broken and upside down in relation to God's kingdom and He calls us to adjust ourselves to right side up living), confess it and ask Him to renew your mind, so that you won't conform to the patterns/ways of this world, but rather be transformed - walking in his good, pleasing and perfect will. (Romans 12:2).

Ask Him how He wants you to respond to His Word.
Thank Him for the resources He provides for you to respond accordingly.
Thank Him for His strength and presence as He continues to work out TRUTH in your life.
Thank Him for the opportunity to walk in His way - the way of everlasting, abundant life, and the only way to deep soul satisfaction.

AMEN!

Psalm 1 & 2: Listening Guide

Happiness, or blessing, doesn't look like chasing stuff or chasing a feeling. It looks like being *a certain kind of person*.

Two Ways:

1. The Psalms don't paint a picture of one way and different progressions along it; they paint a picture of _____.

2. There are only two ways. There is no third way that _____ the _____ of the two.

3. Two _____ – Matthew 7:13,14 & Psalm 1:6
   Two _____ – Matthew 7:15-20 & Psalm 1:3-4
   Two _____ – Matthew 7:21-23 & Psalm 1:6

Two Ways to Live:

4. The Bible exposes moral weakness and failure because it is the truth of the human condition, but never do we see it _____.

5. How do we avoid the _____ onto the wrong path, and the progression along it? We _____ on the Law of the Lord. We delight in it.

Can you imagine coming to the end of a long journey, only to realize the road you took led you to a dead end and you didn't have the time to backtrack?

View this teaching session at www.unshakenministries.com

6. The word translated _____ in Psalm 2:1 is the same word that is translated _____ in Psalm 1:2.

Psalm 2:10 - We would be wise to heed the warning.
Psalm 2:11 - Warning: Serve the LORD with fear, and rejoice with trembling.

Two Ends:

7. _____ now so you don't _____ later!

8. The true and lasting path to happiness, to blessing, is this: Be the kind of person who takes _____ in the Son.

The ungodly are the reverse of the righteous, both in character and condition.
Matthew Henry

In the fullest sense of the word, to be 'blessed' is more than just being happy. It's being approved. We will ultimately either look for happiness or approval from the world or from God. The path to approval from God is through His Son, Jesus.

9. Thus, the only path that leads to true blessing and lasting happiness is the path that takes us to the _____.

Week Two: Where Is Your Confidence?

One of the things we will be confronting throughout our journey in the Psalms is the tension that exists between emotion and experience. Our experiences will not always lend themselves to constructive or positive emotions. What will we do with this? How do we move forward productively and with focus, acknowledging our feelings rather than simply stuffing them away, but at the same time, not allowing them to lead us on a wild goose chase?

If we want to become women characterised by stability, focus, and confidence, we need a sure hope. Hebrews 6:17-20 tells us that we who have fled to Jesus Christ for refuge have a sure hope. A steadfast anchor for our soul.

This week we will journey through psalms of lament and look at where our confidence lies. All of the psalms this week are written by David, and come from situations of trouble or distress. Yet, we see David maintain confidence despite his circumstances.

---

a WORD to the wise

But as for me, I watch in hope for the LORD,

I wait for God my Saviour;

my God will hear me.

Micah 7:7 NIV

Day One: Answer Me When I Call (Psalm 4)

You know how occasionally something happens and you just have to tell someone? Maybe it's great news and you simply must share it. Maybe it's a burden and you feel like you can't carry it alone.

When my oldest was a baby, everything he did was new to me because he was my firstborn. Overwhelmed with new experiences, I was often filled with a compulsive need to overshare. Sometimes, it was because I had no idea what to do – I desperately needed help. Sometimes it was because I was so excited I couldn't keep it to myself – it was spilling out of me and I needed to spill it onto someone who cared.

One day when he was about six months old, he spent his afternoon taking a long nap. This was a first. He inched past the one-hour mark, then towards the two-hour mark, and then past two hours. I itched to share this great news, but I contained myself scared the sound of my voice would wake him. His cry finally came over the monitor and I bounced up the stairs to his room, ready to coo all over him.

What a sight met my eyes! He'd experienced a diaper blowout of epic proportions. It was everywhere and I had no idea where to start. So what did I do? Well, as a seasoned and experienced mother (sense the sarcasm), I immediately ran for the phone and called my husband.

As soon as his familiar hello came across the line, I launched into a graphic description of the situation. I spared no details because I needed someone to be living this with me. Undaunted by the sustained silence on the other end of the phone, I moved through my suspense - how long would he really nap? My elation- he passed the two-hour mark! The horror – what I beheld as I entered his bedroom at the end of it all.

I described his hair, his clothes, his crib. I tried to make the experience multi-sensory by including graphic descriptions of the smell.

All to silence.

Finally, I interrupted my own monologue to ask Rob if he was still there. Very quietly he informed me that yes, he was there, but he was in an important meeting and couldn't talk.

I was mortified. Very quietly I asked if the people sitting around the table could hear me. Rob says, "Well, honey, you're kind of loud."

I hung up the phone and dealt with my situation. But the whole time I was cleaning up my son, I kept asking myself, why would Rob have picked up the phone if he couldn't talk? If he wasn't really going to listen, why did he waste my time – I could have called someone else?!

At the heart of it though, I was really questioning why I had called in the first place. Was there anything he could have done to help me?

No. I had cried out into silence and I was met by silence.

We've probably all been there. Wanting someone to talk to, but more than that, needing someone to respond.

1. Read Psalm 4.
    a. What is the title of this psalm? (The first five words of it.)

    b. Write down any words or phrases that relate to the title.

    c. Is there any evidence as to how the psalmist expects God to respond to this request? (verse 3)

    d. Do you pray with this same expectation? Why or why not?

2. Read Psalms 3:3-4 and 62:8. Write them in your own words.

3. What does Psalm 3:4 say God will do?

The book of Psalms is unique in that it is a record of the cries of man to God rather than the words of God to man. So can we trust this? Or does this take away some of our confidence? Well, it shouldn't. Because like we said at the beginning of this study, these are still the inspired words of Scripture. Completely trustworthy.

4. What does the prophet Isaiah say in Isaiah 30:19 and 58:9?

All throughout the psalms we see the psalmists cry out to God, and they fully expect Him to hear and to answer!

5. Read Psalm 5:1-3.
   a. Who is the author addressing his cries to in verse 2?

   b. What word comes before each title that is used?

   c. Notice the order of verse 3: what does the author acknowledge first, and how does this shape his response?

6. Read Isaiah 21:6, 8; Habakkuk 2:1, and Micah 7:7: What is the general idea that unites these verses with each other and with Psalm 5:3?

How would your day look different if you began each morning by crying out to God, knowing He hears, and then watching in confident expectation of what He will do?

We started today with a story that showcased my desire and need to run somewhere. We have a place to run. The throne of God. And we can run there with confidence.

Therefore, brothers, since we have confidence to enter the holy places by the blood of Jesus, by the new and living way that he opened for us through the curtain, that is, through his flesh, and since we have a great priest over the house of God, let us draw near with a true heart in full assurance of faith with our hearts sprinkled clean from an evil conscience and

our bodies washed with pure water. Let us hold fast the confession of our hope without wavering, for he who promised is faithful.

Hebrews 10:19-23 ESV

Talking to God:

As you come to the throne of grace, cry out to God in confidence, knowing He hears. Place the details of your situation before Him, and then watch in expectation of what He will do. Friends, this is not a promise of outcome. It is a promise of presence.

O LORD, in the morning you hear my voice;

In the morning I prepare a sacrifice for you and watch. Psalm 5:3 ESV

Day Two: Who Will Show Us Some Good? (Psalm 4)

The opening story yesterday recounted a time that I cried out, but wasn't really heard. We saw that we have One we can cry out to and that He will listen. Crying out to someone who will listen is a great starting point. But it's not the only point or even the end point. Despite Rob's feelings towards me and my situation that day, he was not in a position to help me.

It's one thing to cry out and be heard. But if the one listening doesn't have the power to act, you might receive comfort, but little more. There's more to it than that, though. What if you have the listening ear of a powerful person, but that person doesn't truly love you? Yes, they hear, and they have the power to act, but will the action be trustworthy? What if you know you can cry out to someone who will hear, who has the power to act, and who loves you deeply, *but*, they are not particularly wise? Should you trust their action on your behalf?

Psalm 4 establishes that God will hear us, but this is only beneficial to us if He has the power to act, if He loves us enough to act in our best interests, and if He is wise enough to discern what those best interests are.

1. Let's go back to Psalm 4 and read it again.
    a. Jot down any words or phrases that indicate to you that God has the power to act on our behalf.

    b. Both Psalm 3 and Psalm 5 have been called companion psalms to Psalm 4. How do Psalm 3:3, 5, 7-8, and Psalm 5:10-12, reinforce the power of God to act on our behalf?

We all come to Bible study from different places and for different reasons, so I won't assume that you believe God to be all powerful. However, it's pretty hard to have even a cursory knowledge of the Bible without being aware that God's power is a point Scripture quickly drives home hard, even to a general audience. His mighty deeds in creation, in deliverance, in meting out justice - they boldly showcase His power.

When we probe the dark corners of our heart, how do we believe that God will use His power where we are concerned?

2. Do you believe He will use His power in absolute love and absolute wisdom where you are concerned?
   a. Why or why not?

   b. What factors in your life experience lead you to answer the question the way that you have?

3. Psalm 4:2 asks two different questions. I've given the second question to you in several different versions and one paraphrase so you can hear it being asked different ways:
   How long will you love vain words and seek after lies? (ESV)
   How long will you love what is worthless and aim at deception? (NASB)
   How long will you love delusions and seek false gods? (NIV)
   How long will you lust after lies? How long will you live crazed by illusion? (MSG)
    a. What do you think is really at the heart of this question? What is David asking here?

   b. What false gods/idols do you see in your own life? What are you chasing?

   c. What gratification do these false gods/idols bring?

   d. What detriment can you see in the long term pursuit of these things?

4. The first line of Psalm 4:6 reads, "There are many who say, 'Who will show us some good?'" How do you think this question relates to the question raised in Psalm 4:2?

5. Verse seven raises an important contrast. "You have put more joy in *my* heart than *they* have when their grain and wine abound."

    a. Who is being contrasted here? (Hint: Look back at verse 3.)

    b. What is the message?

We have come to the heart of the matter. Those who seek after false gods may well have a pay off in this lifetime. They may experience material prosperity and even a measure of joy. Those who pursue God have joy in their heart, but they are not guaranteed prosperity or ease.

If we are honest, in the dark hours of the night while we are pondering on our beds alone and in the quiet, does this bother us? Does this make us angry because it seems like a poor trade off? Yes, I have God and inner peace, but they have an easier time of it here and now.

Who are we looking to, to show us some good, and what do we perceive as the 'good'?

The LORD spoke to Moses, saying, "Speak to Aaron and his sons, saying, Thus you shall bless the people of Israel: you shall say to them,

The LORD bless you and keep you;

the LORD make his face to shine upon you and be gracious to you;

the LORD lift up his countenance upon you and give you peace.

"So shall they put my name upon the people of Israel, and I will bless them."

Numbers 6:22-27 ESV

In Psalm 4, David is in troubling circumstances. He knows there are many who say, "show us some good." David recalls the blessing God put upon His people. He cries out to God to lift up the light of His face upon them. David sees that he has greater joy in his heart, but they have grain and wine in abundance. The people who are chasing false gods see tangible evidence. The followers of Yahweh, at this time, do not.

We may believe that God hears. We may believe that He has the power to act. But will we believe that He is acting in love and wisdom on our behalf even when the evidence doesn't back this up?

Then my enemies will turn back in the day when I call. This I know, that God is for me. Psalm 56:9 ESV

Day Three: Song of the Sinner (Psalms 6)

We have seen the confidence of the psalmist David this week. He has confidence God hears him when he calls, and he is confident God has the power to act on his behalf and that He will do so in love and wisdom. Today we come to Psalm 6, which is one of the penitential psalms – the prayer of a sinner.

In Psalm 6, we see that sinful humanity can come before a Holy God with confidence.

If that sentence doesn't blow your socks off, you are either too complacent about how Holy God is, or you are too blind to your own sin. I know that sounds pretty harsh, but it's the truth.

Throughout the Old Testament, when man encounters God, he ends up on His face. An example of this is in Isaiah 6, the story of Isaiah's encounter with God. He sees just the train of God's robe fill the temple - the temple was massive. The foundation shakes and the temple fills with smoke at the voice of God. Isaiah responds with, "Woe is me! For I am lost; for I am a man of unclean lips, and I dwell in the midst of a people of unclean lips; for my eyes have seen the King, the LORD of hosts!" (Is. 6:5) Isaiah encounters God and sees himself with great clarity.

1. Begin by reading Psalm 6. If you can, read it out loud and from several different versions. (I start in the ESV, but really like the NKJV for this one.) Note words or phrases that stand out to you as perhaps being important to understanding the psalm.

2. What does David ask God NOT to do in verse 1?

3. What does David ask God to do in verse 2?

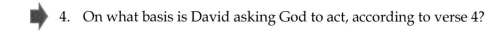 4. On what basis is David asking God to act, according to verse 4?

David acknowledges that he is guilty, but he is asking for grace. Do you think this is a flippant request?

 5. Read Psalm 143:2. Do you think David has an accurate view of God's holiness and his own sinfulness? Explain.

It seems clear that David knew who God was and who he was. The basis of David's request for mercy in Psalm 6:4 is critical and is referred to consistently throughout the psalms. It is rooted in something far more trustworthy than a feeling.

6. Quickly read Psalm 6:4 to remind yourself the basis of David's request for mercy, and then flip back to Psalm 5:7. On what basis does David come into the presence of God?

David's confidence in being heard by God, in being able to enter the presence of God, and in being extended grace by God, are all rooted in who God has said that He is.

Knowledge of God's promises gives us confidence.

David knows the history of his people. Centuries before David's time, Moses was told to lead the people of God into the Promised Land but God hadn't yet said if He was going with them. Moses' response to God is, "if you don't go with us, I'm not going either. I don't want anything, even something as wonderful as the Promised Land, if I have it apart from you." Doesn't that sound like Moses knew Who was going to show him some good?!

God is pleased with Moses' answer, so Moses prevails upon the favour of God to ask for a favour of his own. He asks God to show him who He is.

7. Read Exodus 34:5-10.
   a. Who is God saying He is?

   b. What is He saying He will do?

This declaration of God's character and intention is the basis of David's confidence. He is not confident in himself or his position, and he was the king of God's chosen people! David is confident in who God is.

    8.   Read Psalm 6:8-9: What is the conclusion to this penitential psalm?

The song of the sinner can be turned to a hymn of praise. Why? Because of the gospel.

    9.   Spend some time writing a psalm of your own. Praise God for who He has revealed Himself to be in His Word and ask Him to give you an accurate view of your own sinfulness. Thank Him for His grace, His love, and His mercy. Thank Him for enduring death on the cross so that you might have life.

In his book titled, <u>Prayer: Experiencing Awe and Intimacy with God,</u> Timothy Keller writes, "The only time in all the gospels that Jesus Christ prays to God and doesn't call him Father is on the cross, when he says, "My God, my God, why have you forgotten me? Why have you forsaken me?" Jesus lost his relationship with the Father so that we could have a relationship with God as father. Jesus was forgotten so that we could be remembered forever – from everlasting to everlasting."[1]

This cry of Jesus came at the ninth hour. The hour when Jews would have offered the evening sacrifice. Jesus was the new, the better, the once-and-for-all sacrifice that put an end to the entire sacrificial system. He is our confidence.

Therefore, brothers, since we have confidence to enter the holy places by the blood of Jesus, by the new and living way that he opened for us through the curtain, that is, through his flesh, and since we have a great priest over the house of God, let us draw near with a true heart in full assurance of faith with our hearts sprinkled clean from an evil conscience and our bodies washed with pure water. Let us hold fast the confession of our hope without wavering, for he who promised is faithful.

Hebrews 10:19-23 ESV

Talking to God:

As you come to the throne of grace today, know that because God did not answer on the day that Jesus cried, He will answer you.

And can it be that I should gain, an interest in the Saviour's blood?

Died He for me, who caused His pain? For me, who Him to death pursued?

Amazing love! How can it be that Thou, my God, shouldst die for me?

He left His Father's throne above, so free, so infinite His grace;

---

[1] Timothy Keller, *Prayer: Experiencing Awe and Intimacy With God*, (Penguin Group (USA) LLC, New York NY, 2014), 80.

Emptied Himself of all but love, and bled for Adam's helpless race;

'Tis mercy all immense and free; For O my God, it found out me.

No condemnation now I dread; Jesus, and all in Him is mine!

Alive in Him, my living Head, and clothed in righteousness divine.

Bold I approach the eternal throne, and claim the crown through Christ my own.

Amazing love! How can it be? That Thou, my God shouldst die for me!

Charles Wesley, 1738

Day Four: O LORD, Deliver My Life (Psalm 6)

My family went to church. Every Sunday. Every Wednesday. Every time there was an evening service, we were there. If we awoke to the misfortune of feeling sick on a Sunday morning, well, what better place to go to feel better than church?

There was no special service for children; young and old were expected to sit through the entire service silent and still. Having attended several times a week for my entire life, I was well-prepared for the pre-teen privilege that was leaving my parents to sit with friends. I had trained for an entire decade for this.

Now, lest you think we were allowed to sit at the back of the church or in the balcony far from watchful eyes, that was not the case. Our first taste of freedom was sitting on rows of chairs lined up on the stage behind the pulpit. Yes. All eyes would be trained on the pastor and we were sitting behind him. Nothing was hidden.

Being on display for all to see should have resulted in perfect behaviour, right? Well, it didn't. For some reason, we managed to trick ourselves into thinking that we could hide. We fooled ourselves into believing we could cover up the giggling, passing notes, tickling (?!), and chatter. We thoroughly enjoyed our freedom until the moment of eye contact.

We were naïve enough to think that if we weren't looking at our parents, they weren't looking at us. But they were watching. They saw. And in the moment we allowed our eyes to make contact with Mom or Dad, we knew the game was up. They had seen all.

From that point on, everything changed. We abandoned our silliness and listened to the pastor like our lives depended on it. We prayed with great reverence, trying to find the correct balance between a little bit of Spirit-led charisma and too much, which would only lead to more trouble later. We sang hymns with gusto.

The threat of imminent discipline modified our behaviour. For that Sunday. Unfortunately, this was not a one-time occurrence. Why didn't getting caught once, ensure there wouldn't be a repeat of this bad behaviour? And why, oh why, did our parents keep letting us enter this minefield of testing?

If our parents could foresee how the situation would play out (and now that I'm a parent, I realize they saw it far better than I did) why didn't they save us from a situation that would likely lead to discipline?

We saw yesterday that Psalm 6 is the song of a sinner.

1. Read Psalm 6: In verse one, what is David asking of God?

 a. Is David saying not to do it at all, or not to do it in a certain way?

b. In verses 4 and 5, what is David asking of God and what is his reason for asking? Try to explain his reason in your own words.

We come to verse 5 and must remember that we are reading poetry. Poetry makes use of images and pictures to convey deeper truths.

Why do we fear death? Why should we fear death?

 2. What do Proverbs 15:11a and Psalm 139:8 say about Sheol?

God is sovereign over death. But death is an end. Death is silence. Plans have ended. Words are done.

 3. How do the words of Hebrews 9:27 and John 9:4 speak to the impact that imminent and certain death should have on our lives?

Death marks the end of God's saving intervention in our lives.

For God to remember is for God to act. (You can check out Genesis 8:1 and 30:22 for examples of this.) As long as God gives us life, He reveals Himself to us and gives us the opportunity to respond to Him. While we are alive, we are able to call out to God who will hear, remember, and act. Death brings our ability to reach out to God and to relate to God to an end. Death is the point where God's saving intervention in our lives comes to an end.

This is where the Gospel comes in. The good news is that because of the work Christ did for us on the cross, God will remember those who come to Him, forever! (Flip back to the end of yesterday's homework and read the quote from Tim Keller (page 35) - Jesus was forgotten by God on the cross so that we could be remembered forever.)

We don't know how complete David's understanding was of what would happen after death, remember, he was a follower of God pre-Christ, but we do know that he had both confidence in the character of God alongside a serious view of the reality of death. That's why in verse 4 he reminds God of the commitment He made but follows it with verse 5, an acknowledgment that remembrance of that commitment ends with death. These are sobering words. That is why verses 6 and 7 show us David crying his eyes out. Weak and wasting away from grief.

4. Read Proverbs 15:11. Write down the second phrase of the verse.

   a. What is the message here? (See also 1 Samuel 16:7.)

   b. Do you find you're more concerned with and aware of your outward behaviour than the inner motives of your heart? Explain.

5. Read Proverbs 3:5-6, 11-12, and Jeremiah 10:23-24. How are we to live according to these passages?

   a. Why does the Lord discipline?

   b. What should our response to God's discipline be?

   c. In what ways have you seen God's discipline to be both loving and good?

Why did my parents keep giving me chances? Why did they discipline again and again, and then let me step out to try one more time? Because they loved me. And they were working through the process of 'how long?' The 'how long' is to grow us.

My son, do not regard lightly the discipline of the Lord, nor be weary when reproved by him. For the Lord disciplines the one he loves, and chastises every son whom he receives. It is for discipline that you have to endure. God is treating you as sons. For the moment all discipline seems painful rather than pleasant, but later it yields the peaceful fruit of righteousness to those who have been trained by it. Therefore lift your drooping hands and strengthen your weak knees, and make straight paths for your feet, so that what is lame may not be put out of joint but rather be healed.

Hebrews 12:5-7, 11-13 ESV

God disciplines us for our own good so that we can share in His holiness. Discipline is not to make us weak but to bring us healing.

While we are alive, God is intervening in our lives to bring about our holiness. That is good news. That is the best news. Even when it hurts.

Psalm 119:67 says, "Before I was afflicted I went astray, but now I keep your word." As humans, we are slow learners and if we think we are getting away with our sin, we will not learn. And so, because of His commitment to love us, He keeps teaching us the lessons. Even when they hurt.

Talking to God:

Proverbs 15:11 tells us that our hearts lie open before God. Sing the song of the sinner today. Ask God to search you and know you. To try you and test your thoughts. To expose any grievous way in you and to root it out so He can lead you in the way everlasting. (Ps 139)

When we consider the alternative, it is far better to be afflicted in life and remembered for eternity.

Day Five: In You I Take Refuge (Psalm 7)

We spent the past two days in a psalm of penitence. David was asking for grace because he needed it. He was begging for deliverance and his appeal was based on the steadfast love of God, not on his own righteousness. There are times we experience weariness, grief, and suffering because God is lovingly trying to get our attention and draw us back to Himself.

However, there are times we experience pain, sorrow, and difficulty because we are broken people living in a broken world. There are times when, like Job, we can experience physical sickness and pain, loss of material possessions and prosperity, and loss of those we love, even though we have been righteous before God.

1. Read through Psalm 7.
    a. What does David ask of God in verse 1?

    b. What evidence is there that David's trouble is not due to sin in his life?

    c. Does God answer David's prayer in this Psalm?

    d. What is David's response as he waits for God to answer (verse 17)?

This week we have been examining where our confidence lies. We have seen that God hears us. We have been reminded that He has the power to act and His actions will be grounded in infinite love and wisdom. Even though we are sinful people, we have confidence because of the sacrifice of Jesus.

What do we do when this doesn't appear to be true? What do we do when it doesn't look like God will save? When it appears He does not hear? When it seems He will not act?

Where will you go when you or someone you love is suffering? Despite best intentions, this is not the time to throw a Romans 8:28 'God is working everything out for your good' bomb in someone's face. This is not the time to glibly remind a sufferer that things will turn out.

God is working things out for good - for ultimate good. If we read past Romans 8:28 and continue to verse 29, we see that our ultimate good is to be conformed to the image of His Son.

But His Son, Jesus, our brother, suffered greatly. He was accused, even though He was perfect. He was mocked and scorned, and He remained silent. He was beaten, humiliated, and killed as a criminal, even though He was the only innocent man who has ever lived.

This is the image we are being conformed to. This is how God is working for our good.

When our confidence is met by silence and perceived inaction, can we still trust God?

There was a man in the land of Uz whose name was Job, and that man was blameless and upright, one who feared God and turned away from evil.

Job 1:1 ESV

Job is the story of a godly man. He was healthy and prosperous. And he lost it all. His family. His possessions. His health. His friends. He lost everything but his life.

Job asked the question: where is God? Job says if I could find God, I would question Him. I would lay my case before Him and argue through all of it. In Job 23:5-7, Job says if I could find Him, I know He would hear me and answer me. He would pay attention to me. (Job 23:6) Job is convinced that if a righteous man could come before the seat of God, he would be allowed to argue his case and the result would be an acquittal by the Judge.

2. Read Job 23:8-9, and 11-12. What is Job saying?

3. Read Job 25:4-6. As he attempts to make sense of the situation, how does Job's friend respond to Job's claim?

4. Read Job 27:1-6. How does Job respond to his friend's attempt to help?

Job is adamant, I have searched my heart and I maintain my innocence. I've done my part, why isn't He doing His?

What do we do with a God we cannot understand?

> **But He is unchangeable, and who can turn Him back?**
>
> **What He desires, that He does.**
>
> **For He will complete what He appoints for me, and many such things are in His mind.**
>
> **Job 23:13-14 ESV**

5. Read Job 23:15-17.
   a. How does Job feel? (verses 15-16)

   b. In a time of turbulence and suffering, does Job allow his feelings to dictate his actions? (verse 17)

   c. Why or why not? (Job 23:10)

6. Read Job 27:8-9: What hope is Job clinging to?

When life seems like a puzzle and the pieces don't fit together, where will you go?

> **But where shall wisdom be found? And where is the place of understanding?**
>
> **Man does not know its worth, and it is not found in the land of the living.**
>
> **For where, then, does wisdom come? And where is the place of understanding?**
>
> **God understands the way to it, and he knows its place. For he looks to the ends of the earth and sees everything under the heavens.**
>
> **And He said to man,**
>
> **'Behold, the fear of the Lord, that is wisdom, and to turn away from evil is understanding.'**
>
> **Job 28:20, 12-13, 23, 28 ESV**

Life isn't easy. It's hard to understand. But our best starting point is to know where to find the place of wisdom and understanding.

The conclusion of Job's story is that he heard from God. God didn't answer the why of the situation. God basically says, You're asking all these questions but they're the wrong questions. You're asking why and the answer is who. (Job 38 to 41 are God's wonderfully poetic response to Job.)

Job doesn't get the answer he was originally looking for, but his response to God was, though my mind can't understand the what, my eyes have glimpsed the who, and you are enough! (Read it in Job 42:1-6.)

7. In the pressure and stress of your life circumstances, is knowing who God is enough for you? Explain.

 8. How does David describe God in Psalm 7:11?

9. When you think of God as a judge, what do you picture?

a. Is this image comforting? Explain.

We will see on our journey through the Psalms, that while we tend to associate the word 'judge' with condemnation, the psalmists see it more as an indication of saving action. They see it more as an act of deliverance; God coming to put the whole world back into its right order. God intervening on behalf of the innocent. God taking the side of the oppressed. God stepping in to save.

God is the one who searches minds and hearts; they are open before Him. We can trust Him to judge rightly. If we search out our hearts and find sin, we must heed the warning in Psalm 7:12. The warning is dire but there is comfort in that we are given the opportunity to repent.

But when your life is a mess and God seems silent, even though you feel like you can stand before Him in integrity, take comfort in the promise that He "has fixed a day on which He will judge the world in righteousness by a man whom He has appointed; and of this He has given assurance to all by raising Him from the dead." (Acts 17:31)

Jesus Christ is a righteous judge. He clothes those who seek refuge in Him with His own righteousness. He promised, "When I am lifted up from the earth, I will draw all people to myself." (John 12:32 ESV)

Talking to God:

Our time today was personal. There are inner workings of the heart known only to God and to us. I don't know the depth of your heart situation, but He does. Pour it out to Him. It's okay to question Him like Job did. It's okay to shout in the face of silence. My prayer is that in your cries, you will come to a place where you can say with Job, "He knows the way that I take; when he has tried me, I shall come out as gold.'

My shield is with God, who saves the upright in heart. Psalm 7:10 ESV

CALL TO PRAYER

Today as I sit to write, reflecting on my own journey with developing confidence in God, my phone keeps chirping with incoming texts requesting prayer. A child bleeding, a father dying, a marriage flailing, a friend betraying, a heart crying, words cutting. Empty, lonely, hurting, sad and anxious souls. What do we do with all of this emotion?

I am reminded of pieces of my own journey. Looking back, I can see the Lord's faithful hand, however, when I was in the middle of the 'waiting room' of apparent silence, darkness, unknown answers, I couldn't see much of anything through the blurred vision my tears caused. Days I dreaded getting out of bed to face the realities and losses and abandonment I felt, caused me to stumble around all the while crying out, "Where are You in all of THIS, God? Do You not see me? Do You not care? If this is what You have in store for me, I'd rather You call me home to Yourself. If it's here that You would have me remain, then You are going to have to carry me through every minute of every day because there is NO way I can spend my days enduring this meaningless existence."

I realized I was at a crossroads of faith and was moved, even in the seemingly silent response, to open my Bible - right at the very beginning, to write down every revelation about who God was and what promises He made to His people and how they responded to Him. It didn't take any time at all to come up with my lifeline prayer, which I prayed many, many times throughout each day: "God, You are good, God, You love me. Thank You."

Then I began to worship, not necessarily with great joy, but what felt more like a "sacrifice of praise." I acknowledged my muddled and even selfish feelings before Him (as He revealed them to be such) and confessed these things to Him. I whined and complained and resisted and submitted and confessed and cried. I sought Him and fell on my knees and began to thank Him for His goodness and love, even though I couldn't see or "feel" it.

And... then... a person, a word spoken in an unexpected place from an unexpected (even unwelcome) source. A choice: be angry or trust that God was at work in unlikely, desolate places, healing, drawing me, loving me, wooing. Revelations while reading the Word, while weeding in the garden, while shopping, while crying through collective worship, while serving the very ones who hurt me. And... finally, an answer to my soul's lament that He would have to carry me through each and every minute of this life that He was asking me to live, to this road He had me trudging on. I sensed Him lovingly say to me, "Of course, Dear One, that's exactly what I have always wanted to do for you." I realized that what He wanted most from me was full dependence, regardless of my situation; whether I was in the worst of days or the best of days. He showed me again His eternal perspective and that my hope is in Him alone (Psalm 33:20, Psalm 20:7, Micah 7:7, Isaiah 26:4).

In Exodus 33:22-23 (NIV), God tells Moses: "When my glory passes by, I will put you in a cleft in the rock and cover you with my hand until I have passed by. Then I will remove my hand and you will see my back." Ann Voskamp in her book, One Thousand Gifts, says,

Is that it? When it gets dark, it's only because God has tucked me in a cleft of the rock and covered me, protected with His hand? ...maybe this is true reality: It is in the dark that God is passing by... Dark is the holiest ground, the glory passing by. In the blackest, God is closest, at work, forging His perfect and right will. Though it is black and we can't see and our world seems to be free-falling and we feel utterly alone, Christ is most present to us... Then He will remove His hand. Then we will look. Then we look back and see His back.[2]

Have you been there, too? In the dark? Are you there right now? Attending Bible Study, offering sacrifices of praise and discipline, and you struggle to see His hand in your life? Dear, dear friend, just maybe you can't see His hand because it is holding you in the cleft of the Rock. (And remember, Christ is our Rock!) Only when you look back (even if it's a long time from now or on the other side of eternity), will you see His back after He's passed by. Oh, Sister, God IS good and He loves you oh so very much, even in your darkest times. The darkness cannot separate you from His love, even when the enemy would have you believe it (Romans 8:39).

Practice
Test me, LORD, and try me, examine my heart and my mind; for I have always been mindful of your unfailing love and have lived in reliance on your faithfulness. Psalm 26: 2 & 3 NLT

Pray through the following questions, seeking the Lord's revelation to you regarding who He is and who He says you are and how He wants you to respond to that knowledge.
Do I believe that He hears my prayers? Do I believe that He has the power to act? Do I believe that He loves me enough to act in my best interest? Do I believe that He is wise enough to discern what my best interests are? Do I believe it always, or only when things are going my way? Do I pray with expectation (Psalm 5:3) and with a heart willing to sacrifice? Do I offer worship and praise despite circumstances that are not ideal? Am I looking only for the promise of an outcome when I pray, or the promise of His presence? Will I make the choice to trust even when I cannot understand? (Isaiah 55:9)

On Our Knees
Read and pray through Psalm 77 NLT
I cry out to God; yes, I shout. Oh, that God would listen to me! When I was in deep trouble, I searched for the Lord. All night long I prayed, with hands lifted toward heaven, but my soul was not comforted. I think of God, and I moan, overwhelmed with longing for his help. You don't let me sleep. I am too distressed even to pray! I think of the good old days, long since ended, when my nights were filled with joyful songs. I search my soul and ponder the difference now. Has the Lord rejected me forever? Will he never again be kind to me? Is his unfailing love gone forever? Have his promises permanently failed? Has God forgotten to be gracious? Has he slammed the door on his compassion? And I said, 'This is my fate; the Most High has turned his hand against me.' But then I recall all you have done, O LORD; I remember your wonderful deeds of long ago. They are constantly in my thoughts. I cannot stop thinking about your mighty works. O God, your ways are holy. Is there any god as mighty as you? You are the God of great wonders! You demonstrate your awesome power among the nations. By your strong arm, you redeemed your people, the descendants of Jacob and Joseph. When the Red Sea saw you, O God, its waters looked and trembled! The sea quaked to its very depths. The clouds poured down rain; the thunder rumbled in the sky. Your arrows of lightning flashed. Your thunder roared from the whirlwind;

---

[2] Ann Voskamp, *One Thousand Gifts* (Zondervan, Grand Rapids, Michigan, 2010), 156.

the lightning lit up the world! The earth trembled and shook. Your road led through the sea, your pathway through the mighty water - a pathway no one knew was there! You led your people along that road like a flock of sheep, with Moses and Aaron as their shepherds. Amen!

We have our own Good Shepherd to lead us through our darkest times. We are hidden in Him - our eternal Rock. While God's glory may pass behind us, so that we only can see Him when we look back, our great hope is in knowing that one day we WILL see Him face to face and ALL WILL be made right.

Psalm 11: Listening Guide

Are You Going to Run?

1. What am I running _____? What am I running _____?

2. "In the LORD I take refuge!" Who is David _____ to? His enemies? God? _____?

Faithless vs Faithful:

3. What are you going to do when your _____ are destroyed?

4. God will have the last word! The LORD is in _____ holy temple; the LORD's _____ is in heaven!

5. Things that can be shaken, will be shaken to be _____. To make way for that which _____ be shaken! (Hebrews 12:27-28)

6. The Full Assurance of Faith: It is _____ - the price is paid. The One who promised is _____. (Hebrews 10)

View this teaching session at www.unshakenministries.com

Something Better:

7. The Faithful know _____ is going to show them the _____ !

8. Don't throw away your _____ - faith has a _____!

9. I will _____ that my help comes from the _____!

10. The Test: It shows what you _____. It shows what you've _____. It shows what you've _____ to learn.

11. All powerful God is a refuge who _____, and who _____ in Love and Wisdom.

12. David opens this psalm with an acknowledgment based on _____. He ends it with sure hope rooted in _____.

Week Three: This God He is Our God

Last week we moved through psalms which, though they were psalms of lament, projected confidence and sure hope. The psalmist was not confident in his circumstances or himself; he was confident in his God. A God who was personal to him.

This week, we are going to go a little deeper into who is our God. We have a sure hope in Him, and there is no greater way to grow our confidence than to gaze upon His face.

---

a WORD to the wise

You will keep in perfect peace him whose mind is steadfast

because he trusts in you. Trust in the LORD forever for the LORD,

the LORD, is the Rock eternal.

Isaiah 26:3-4 NIV

Day One: The Law of the LORD Is Perfect (Psalm 19)

Have you ever poured yourself out for someone you loved? I mean, laid bare your heart: who you really are and what drives your affections?

I was a teenager before the internet age of instant communication. My friends and I communicated in person, via phone calls, and by writing notes. And boy, did we write notes. Should the English teacher require us to write a five-page essay, there would be loud laments. But writing a five-page note in different colours of ink to pour out our feelings? We easily pulled that off in one class. (That was while taking the time to dot all i's with little hearts and turn all o's into smiley faces.)

Love notes propelled this art form to a whole new level. Colour of ink was chosen intentionally. Song lyrics and poetry sprinkled liberally. Metaphor and imagery which would have delighted our teachers, prevailed successful. (Well, mostly.) These pages attempted to convey, "This is who I am. Could you love me? Do you love me still?"

The process of falling in love involves revealing yourself to the one you love as trust grows. Love seeks to uncover.

I was excited to come to Psalm 19, because it is a familiar psalm to me. Like a love note, softened with repeated reading, I came to it anticipating a comfortable tenderness. Sort of like this one note I remember from high school. I thought I understood the gist of it. And I did. But not the depth of it. The note referenced a song. I didn't bother checking out the song lyrics because I thought the title kind of gave it away. One day as I was going over the note again, I decided to check out the song. As I listened to the lyrics, I realized the author of the note had been saying something far deeper than I had been hearing.

This week we are gazing more intently upon the face of God. We will not be disappointed. As we see the One who reveals Himself to us, our love will grow. Our trust will deepen. And our faith will be strengthened.

1. Read Psalm 19:1-6.

   a. What are the verbs in verses 1 and 2?

   b. What is 'speaking' in verses 1-4? (Hint: 'what' not 'who.')

   c. How far-reaching is the voice referred to in verse 4?

   d. Finish the following phrases in capital letters: *The heavens declare the* _____, *and the sky above proclaims* _____. *(ESV)*

   e. Who and/or what is the focus of this opening section?

   f. What is the implication of this for you?

2. Now read Psalm 19:7-9.

   a. What name of God is used in these three verses and how many times does it appear?

   b. What is the subject of these verses? (There are many synonyms listed.)

   c. What six words are used to describe the subject?

   d. The subject will work six effects. What are they?

3. Read Psalm 19:10-11.

    a. The subject of these two verses is the same as the subject in verses 7-9. How is the subject described in these two verses?

    b. Taken from the ESV again, fill in the blanks: *Moreover, by them is your servant _____; in keeping them there is great _____.*

4. Read the conclusion of Psalm 19 in verses 12-14, filling in the blanks: *Who can discern his errors? Declare me innocent from _____ faults. Keep back your servant also from presumptuous sins; let them not have _____ over me! Then I shall be _____, and innocent of great transgression. Let the words of my mouth and the meditation of my heart be acceptable in your sight, O LORD, my rock and my _____.* *(ESV)*

Did you notice that the psalm is divided into three parts that become increasingly narrow? The first six verses are broad and expansive – all of creation and the ends of the earth. Verses seven through eleven narrow down. Creation boldly shouts in generalities; the law speaks to specifics.

The law of the LORD reveals more of who our God is. While the first six verses use the term 'God,' and only once, the next five verses use the personal name of God: Yahweh - Covenant God, and they use it six times.

The final three verses zoom in even closer. They are the words of a specific type of people. The heart cry of those who have attended to the voice that is spoken for all to hear.

The conclusion of Psalm 19 contains the words of one who has gazed upon the law of the LORD and has seen it to be desirable.

5. Do you see the law of the Lord as sweet, good, and desirable? Why or why not?

In the first week of homework, we discussed the fact that God has always existed and that He does not change. His law is a reflection of Him. Therefore, it is merciful of Him to reveal His law to us because it shows us who He is and how to be in relationship with Him.

 6. The book of Exodus spends a lot of time describing the law and how the people of God were to fulfill it. What was the purpose of all the regulations God gave His people according to Exodus 29:42-46?

In Psalm 19, we see the psalmist exploring the mind-blowing magnificence of God's creation. But he saw that there was something even more wonderful than that.

There was opportunity for intimacy with the Creator.

The words of God are a little bit like my high school letters. I tended to think the letters I received were for me, therefore they were about me. However, more often than not, the letters were more about the authors. They were more about revealing who they were. God's Word is for us, and it is about us, but it is far more about Him. He is revealing Himself to us so that we can know Him and enter into relationship with Him. As we learn more about Him, we will learn more about ourselves, but we will miss the grandness and intention of the Bible if we make it a book about us.

Talking to God:

As you enter into the presence of Creator God today, meditate on the magnificence of His creation and what it reveals of Him. Meditate on the wonder of His law – His righteous standard revealed. Thank God that you can experience intimacy with our wonderful Creator who is both high and lifted up, yet mindful of us.

Day Two: My Redeemer Lives (Psalm 19)

Yesterday I told you about a love note I received in high school. For weeks I savoured the note, thinking I had plumbed its depths. One day, I decided to listen to the song the author spoke of, only to discover the note was far deeper and richer than I had previously understood.

Psalm 19 presents a similar scenario. The language of the psalm is intended to turn the reader back to the story of creation. It was something I had known for a while, but I hadn't taken the time to go back and read the opening chapters of Genesis in this context.

Because, much like that high school love note, I thought I understood the gist of it. God created. The work of His hand was big and beautiful. That is the gist of it. Yes, but that is not the depth of it.

Let's go back to the beginning and see what is being revealed to us by the Author.

1. Begin today by re-reading Psalm 19 and making note of words, phrases, or images you think the author used to turn us back to the Creation account in Genesis.

2. Read Genesis 1:1, 1:26-28, 31, 2:8-9, 2:15-17. (I tried to pick verses that would condense the creation story in the interest of time, but if you want to read the story in detail, read all of Genesis 1 and 2.) NOTE: Questions like the ones below are not intended simply for

busy work. They are intended to encourage attention to specific details because we are quick to skim over what we think is familiar.

    a.   In whose image was man made in Genesis 1:26?

    b.   What was man to have dominion over? (Notice the last phrase of verse 26.)

    c.   How were the trees in the garden described in Genesis 2:9?

    d.   What two trees were placed in the midst of the garden?

    e.   What command did God give to man in Genesis 2:16-17?

    f.   What would be the result of breaking that command?

3.   Read Genesis 3:1-13.

    a.   Who (or what) initiates the scene in Chapter 3?

    b.   According to Genesis 1:26 and question 2b, what should have been the nature of the relationship between the woman and the serpent?

    c.   What does the serpent say to the woman in Genesis 3:5, and what is ironic about this, considering what was said in Genesis 1:26-27?

    d.   In what ways do you see Satan shifting your gaze so that your focus is on what you don't have instead of on what you have been blessed with?

God created. As the Creator, He had a specific plan and order, rules for how His creation would work. He revealed this plan to mankind. He gave mankind the responsibility of governing the earth on His behalf. Having done this, God did not just dust off His hands, congratulate Himself on a job well done, and disappear. Creator God walked with humanity in His creation.

4. Compare the way the tree is described in Genesis 3:6 with the way the law of the LORD is described in Psalm 19:10.

5. Compare what Psalm 19:7b and 8b say about what the law of the LORD does, and what the serpent told the woman the fruit would do in Genesis 3:5.

6. In Psalm 19:9b, what does the psalmist say about the rules of the LORD and how does this compare with what the woman tells God the serpent did to her in Genesis 3:13?

7. In the second phrase of Psalms 19:13, the psalmist prays, asking that sin will not what?

   a. What was the intended role of mankind according to Genesis 1:26?

   b. What are you allowing to have dominion in your life?

For what can be known about God is plain to them, because God has shown it to them. For His invisible attributes, namely, His eternal power and divine nature, have been clearly perceived, ever since the creation of the world, in the things that have been made. So they are without excuse. For although they knew God, they did not honour Him as God or give thanks to Him, but they became futile in their thinking, and their foolish hearts were darkened. Claiming to be wise, they became fools, and exchanged the glory of the immortal God for images resembling mortal man and birds and animals and creeping things.

Therefore, God gave them up in the lusts of their hearts to impurity, to the dishonouring of their bodies among themselves, because they exchanged the truth about God for a lie and worshipped and served the creature rather than the Creator, who is blessed forever! Amen.

Romans 1:19-25 ESV

Creator God proclaims Himself through His creation - the heavens declare the glory of God. But rather than worship the One they point to, we get caught up worshipping the objects themselves.

Yahweh, Covenant God, reveals His instructions to humanity. "Do not eat from this tree or you will die." He gives His law to His people for their own good. To preserve us and give us life. (Deuteronomy 6:24-25) We see it as restrictive. We buy the lie of the serpent, thinking we can do what we want and we won't die.

8. Read Genesis 3:21: How did God respond?

God restored what was broken.

Those garments of skin had to come from something which had once been alive. Life was sacrificed for fellowship to be restored. In love, God covered up that which had been exposed.

Restoration was bought through sacrifice.

For God so loved the world, that He gave His only Son . . .

Talking to God:

Lord, great wonders workest Thou!

To Thy sway all creatures bow; Write Thou deeply in my heart

What I am, and what Thou art!

Joachim Neander, 1650-1680

Day Three: The LORD Is My Shepherd (Psalm 23)

We come today to a psalm so familiar that most people can quote large portions of it, even if they are unfamiliar with the rest of the Bible. Psalm 23 is a most personal psalm of David. Warrior David had written of God as a shield and a fortress. David the fugitive had written of God as a refuge and a rock. But in this psalm, David, who lived with sheep before living in a palace, picks up his pen and writes, "Yahweh is my shepherd."

The man who protected his sheep from fierce predators crafts a song of confidence in his Shepherd's care. The man who provided for the most basic needs of his sheep - food and water - sings a song of trust in his Shepherd's provision. The man who rubbed oil on sheep wool and skin to heal and protect, and who bound up wounded sheep and carried them on his shoulders, declares that he, too, has a Shepherd who brings healing. The man who led his sheep safely home on paths they could not see or understand, writes simple yet profound words of peace, contentment, and love for the Shepherd who walks before him.

1. Let's start with a broad reading of Psalm 23 before we narrow our focus.
    a. What pronoun comes before the word 'shepherd' in verse 1?

b. Verse one makes two statements. What is the first statement? What does the second statement say is true because the first is true?

c. According to verses 2 and 3, what will the Shepherd do and why?

d. What situation is the psalmist walking through in verse 4?

e. What statement does he make in the middle of this verse and what is his reasoning for feeling this way?

f. What does God's presence bring David, even in the midst of his chaos?

g. Who is doing the leading in verses 2 and 3?

h. Who is following in verse 6? (You might need to read Exodus 34:5-6 as a reminder. Psalm 139:5 and Isaiah 52:12 are also wonderful companions to Psalm 23:6.)

i. What is the conclusion of the psalm?

Can you see the lines and colour of the picture David is painting of his Shepherd? The picture of a shepherd would have had clear resolution to readers of that day. For us today, the picture is a bit fuzzier.

The image of God as a shepherd crops up all throughout Scripture. To clarify the image, we'll turn to a passage in Ezekiel. God is condemning the leaders of Israel. He's using the metaphor of shepherds and their flock to say Israel's leaders have not led well.

2. Read Ezekiel 34:1-10 and write down in point form what the shepherds were supposed to be doing to care for their sheep.

3. Read Ezekiel 34:11-16: How does God say He will respond to right the situation?

4. In case there is any confusion, Ezekiel 34:31 makes the point clear. Write down the words of this verse.

God is not just David's Shepherd, He is your Shepherd.

Tucked away at the end of Psalm 23:3 is a statement that grounds the trustworthiness of our Shepherd.

5. Write down the last phrase of Psalm 23:3 and then turn to Isaiah 48:11 and write that down as well.

All that God does is grounded in who He is. He cannot be inconsistent. God will make sure that He gets the glory.

To our sin-damaged minds this sounds conceited. It's not. For God to allow His glory to go to another would be fatal. It would be as if someone you deeply loved suffered a lethal bite from a poisonous snake. You know that in your pocket you carry the only anti-venom that could save them. But you don't want to brag. You don't want to appear self-centred. So instead of shouting loudly for all to hear, "I've got the cure - let me at her I can save her!" you stay quiet. Instead of doing whatever it took to get at your loved one and inject the cure, you watch passively while others work to save her. Maybe you even offer false hope or encouragement as you hand the one in need of healing over to death.

God getting all the glory is for our good. It is for our very life.

We can trust our Shepherd.

He will lead us in right paths. Even when paths are through dark valleys. Even when the path is through the darkest valley of all, the valley of death, and no person can walk with you. Your Shepherd walks beside you. He will lead you safely home. We can trust Yahweh – Covenant God – because His name is a promise.

What could we want when this God is our Shepherd?

Talking to God:

The King of love my Shepherd is,

Whose goodness faileth never,

I nothing lack if I am His

And He is mine forever

Henry W. Baker © 1868

Day Four: Goodness and Mercy Follow Me (Psalm 23)

As you worked through Psalm 23 yesterday, you might have read the promises of God, "*I myself will search for my sheep and will seek them out . . . I will feed them with good pasture . . . I myself will make them lie down . . . I will seek the lost, and I will bring back the strayed, and I will bind up the injured, and I will strengthen the weak . . .*" and have wanted the words to be for you.

But maybe past hurts, rejections, or wanderings, tempted you to rationalize that they are not. Maybe you're thinking, "Okay, the words are real. From a real God. To a real people. But the people are Israel. I don't belong."

Not so fast, dear sheep. When God came down to us in the flesh through Jesus, He went to His people. The people of Israel. And He spoke a language they could understand.

1. Begin today by re-reading Psalm 23. Now turn to Genesis 47:3: How did Joseph's brothers describe themselves and their ancestors to Pharaoh?

2. Flip forward a couple of pages to Genesis 48:15. These are the words of Jacob, the man who God re-named Israel - a man who had been a shepherd all his life and was now lying on his deathbed. How does Jacob refer to God?

The patriarchs of God's chosen people were shepherds. When God revealed Himself to His people as their Shepherd, He was coming to them in tender familiarity. When He spoke to Isaiah and said that He would tend his flock like a shepherd and gather the lambs in His arms, that He would carry them in His bosom and gently lead those that are with young (Is 40:11), God was speaking to them in images they would understand.

Because God was planning to come to them in person. And when He came to speak to them in the flesh, He wanted His people to get what He was saying.

3. Write down the words of Jesus in John 10:14.

God came to the lost sheep of Israel. But know this: Jesus knew that those of us outside the people of Israel would come to Him one day, too. He planned it that way.

4. Write down the words of Jesus in John 10:16.

I had three sons before I had my daughter. Let me tell you, right from the start it was obvious that boys and girls are different! One thing my daughter will do, that my sons have never done, is she will go to her room when her feelings are tender. Usually not quietly though. She likes to make it clear that she is there. Do you know why? Because she wants us to pursue her. She wants us to come to her and draw her out of her room and back into our common living area.

I understand what she is doing, because I do it, too. When I'm hurt or lonely, instead of telling my husband what I'm feeling, I become quiet, wanting him to pursue me.

From Genesis to Revelation, God has been pursuing His lost sheep with consistency.

The book of Revelation is the conclusion to the redemption story. Chapter 7 tells of a magnificent vision that begins with a massive crowd of people. John, the one receiving the vision, learns that the crowd is composed of 144,000, those who have been sealed from every tribe of Israel. But the vision doesn't end there.

5. Read Revelation 7:9-10: What does John see in this passage?

6. Read Revelation 7:14: What unites this group?

7. Read Revelation 7:15-17.
   a. What is the Lamb doing according to the last phrase of verse 15?

   b. Because of that, what is the result according to verse 16?

   c. How is the Lamb described in verse 17?

   For the Lamb in the midst of the throne will be my shepherd, and He will guide me to springs of living water, and God will wipe away every tear from my eyes.

The Lord is your Shepherd. The Shepherd to the shepherds in Genesis is the Shepherd who is a Lamb in Revelation.

Talking to God:

Spend some time writing your own psalm today. In what ways is God your shepherd? Praise Him and thank Him for the ways He pursues you, tends you, guides you, and carries you.

Great is Thy faithfulness, O God my Father. There is no shadow of turning with Thee.

Thou changest not, Thy compassions they fail not; As Thou hast been Thou forever wilt be.

Thomas O. Chisholm, 1866-1960

Day Five: My Light and My Salvation (Psalm 27)

Children run to their parents for different reasons at different times. Early interactions tend to be characterised by need. Parents can meet needs that children can't meet for themselves. Parents feed and clothe their children. They provide shelter for them. They are a source of defence and justice.

As children grow parent/child interactions shift. Children begin to see their parents as people, not just parents. They become interested in their thoughts, opinions, and personalities, and come to enjoy spending time together.

As an adult, I have come to enjoy spending time with my parents. But in situations of need, I quickly revert back to a child-like awareness of their role in my life. My dad consistently remains the strong figure I run to for help.

I remember a time I was newly married and living about a thousand kilometers away from my parents and I ran into trouble. My sister and I had gone out for lunch and came back to our car only to find the keys locked inside. I wasn't stressed in the least and didn't even think twice about how to respond. I immediately walked back into the restaurant and called my Dad.

Being the gracious person he is, he listened to me and offered very helpful suggestions before kindly reminding me that I did have a husband who was perhaps a nearer and equally effective source of help.

I was not undone when presented with a problem because I knew I could run to my Father.

When I read Psalm 27, I picture a child talking 'big' because they know their father is standing behind them and he has their back. When the situation turns threatening, the child runs behind their father's legs and maintains confidence from there.

1. Read Psalm 27.
   a. What three things does David say the LORD is to him in verse 1?

   b. Use a dictionary to find and record the definition for the word 'salvation.'

We can infer from the three images of God that David refers to in verse one, that David was in a situation that was dark, and he needed a light. He was bound up in something, and needed a deliverer. He was being pursued and needed somewhere safe to run.

2. Verses 3 and 6 drive this point home.
   a. What is the situation or circumstance of verse 3 and how do David's feelings correspond to it?

b. According to verse 6, where is David, what is surrounding him, and what is he doing?

As you've probably noticed, Psalm 27 is a psalm of confidence and trust. Not because the circumstances lend themselves to this as a feeling, but because the subject of the psalmist's declarations has inspired this as a choice.

We cannot choose our feelings, but we can choose how we will respond to them and what we will do with them. How do we reign in those potentially wild and crazy feelings that can have us running every which way?

Focus.

 3. What is David's one focus according to verse 4?

 4. To maintain his focus, David asks for two things at the end of verse 4. What two things does David hone in on to stay focused? (Hint: look for the two verbs in the last two phrases of verse 4.)

5. What is David doing in verse 8, and which of the two things from last question does this connect to?

6. What is David asking for in verse 11, and which of the two things from question 4 does this connect to?

7. In what ways are you intentionally seeking God and gazing upon His beauty?

Losing focus keeps us from being productive.

The Gospel of Luke records this wonderful story of Jesus' encounter with two women. The two women respond very differently to the exact same situation.

8. Read Luke 10:38-42 from the ESV.
   a. What does Martha do in response to Jesus' visit in verse 38?

b. What does Mary do in response to Jesus' visit in verse 39?

c. What are the first four words of verse 40?

d. Because of Martha's state, what does that lead her to ask Jesus in verse 40? Write down the first five words of her question.

e. What does Jesus say is Martha's problem in verse 41?

f. What is the solution to the problem? (The answer is the first five words of verse 42, which are the last five words of the sentence Jesus started in verse 41.)

g. Are you a Mary or a Martha? Do you seek God first, or are you easily distracted by the busyness of life? Explain.

9. Read the words of Jesus in Luke 12:22-26, 30-34.
   a. According to verses 22 and 25, what are some of the worries that distract us?

   b. What is Jesus' response to these concerns, according to verses 30-32?

   c. Are you content with this response? Explain.

We are getting to know God better this week, seeing Him with more depth and richness. Psalm 27 beautifully shows us levels of relationship with God. We see the joy that a mature relationship with God brings – delighting in Him because He is delightful. But we also see the security that comes from knowing that the One we love and delight in will always be a safe place to run to. He will always have our back.

Ultimately, confidence in God is a trust issue. Trust is the antidote to anxiety.

Psalm 27 closes with a call to confidence. Wait for the LORD. This is not a passive waiting around while your hands are tied. This is the language of entering the promised land.

Have I not commanded you? Be strong and courageous. Do not be frightened, and do not be dismayed, for the LORD your God is with you wherever you go.
Joshua 1:9 ESV

Derek Kidner, in his commentary on the Psalms, says that we may have,

"no more to go on than the assurance that God is worth waiting for. But that is enough."[3]

Talking to God:

Having looked at our God more closely this week, we have seen Him to be Mighty Creator, Redeemer, and Shepherd. We have seen that He is our real, personal, and trustworthy Father. A safe place to run to. The words of the hymn below are a declaration of confidence; they proclaim that, even when we don't understand, we can trust in who He is.Could they be our prayer?

Whate'er my God ordains is right, His holy will abideth;

I will be still, whate'er He doth, and follow where He guideth.

He is my God; though dark my road, He holds me that I shall not fall;

wherefore to Him I leave it all.

Whate'er my God ordains is right, He never will deceive me;

He leads me by the proper path; I know He will not leave me.

I take, content, what He hath sent; His hand can turn my griefs away,

so patiently I wait His day.

Whate'er my God ordains is right, here shall my stand be taken;

though sorrow, need, or death be mine, yet am I not forsaken.

My Father's care is round me there, He holds me that I shall not fall,

and so to Him I leave it all!

Samuel Rodigast, 1649-1708

---

[3] Derek Kidner, *Psalms 1-7: Kidner Classic Commentaries* (Inter-Varsity Press, London, 1973) 139.

DIGGING DEEPER: YAHWEH: What's in a Name?

Names are given to us at birth. They come to be a part of our identity, who we are. Parents put a great deal of thought into choosing names for their children. Meanings are researched. Sentimentality might even play into the name selected. But at the end of the day, for most of us, our names don't define us. They don't reveal character attributes or qualities we possess. They are just a name.

This is not the case with God. Numerous titles and names are given to God in Scripture and each one reveals something about His character, who He is, and what He intends to do. His many names are a way for us to get to know Him intimately.

Those who know Your name put their trust in You.
Psalm 9:10 ESV

If we don't know who God is, how can we trust Him? Trust comes from knowing. Trust comes from believing. And trust comes from relationship. All three must be present. It is not enough to just know Scripture. In John 5:39-40, Jesus says, "You diligently study the Scriptures because you think that by them you possess eternal life. These are the Scriptures that testify about Me, yet you refuse to come to Me to have life." (ESV)

Our knowledge of Scripture must point us to true faith, faith that God will fulfill all His promises through Christ Jesus, His Son. And our knowledge of Scripture must lead us into a deeper level of intimacy with our Father - into relationship with Him. This is where we find life. This is where we find hope. And this is where we find love. Relationship begins with an introduction. It starts with a name. This is also true of our relationship with God.

While there are many names and titles given to God in Scripture, there is only one personal name for God: YAHWEH. YAHWEH is translated LORD (all caps) in most of our Bibles because in Biblical times, the Jews had such reverence for this name of God, they wouldn't speak it aloud for fear of taking the Lord's name in vain. Whenever they saw this name, they would pronounce it *Adonai* instead, meaning, 'my lord.' Many English translations of the Bible have followed this pattern. The problem for us today is that we lose the magnitude of the meaning of YAHWEH with this limited translation LORD.

Let's turn to Scripture and dig a little deeper into the meaning.

A key text for understanding God's personal name is found in Exodus 3:1-17, where the name YAHWEH is introduced for the first time. Moses encounters God in a burning bush. God declares that He has seen the affliction of His people and has come down to rescue them. He tells Moses, "I am sending you to Pharaoh to bring My people the Israelites out of Egypt." Faced with this great task, Moses asks God, "Who do I say You are?" Take a couple of minutes to read God's reply.

GOD'S ANSWER

God tells Moses: "I AM WHO I AM...I AM has sent me to you," "YAHWEH, the God of your fathers – the God of Abraham, the God of Isaac and the God of Jacob – has sent me to you," and "YAHWEH, the God of your fathers...appeared to me and said: I have watched over you and have seen what has been done to you in Egypt. And I have promised to bring you up out of your misery in Egypt into...a land flowing with milk and honey."

God's response reveals some key aspects of His character.

I AM WHO I AM

First, we see in this text that YAHWEH is used interchangeably with I AM. The name is derived from the Hebrew verb meaning to be, to become, to live or to have life. When Moses asks God, "Who are you?" God answers with an authoritative statement, "I AM WHO I AM!" God is saying, "I AM here, I AM alive, I exist. It doesn't matter what your opinion of Me is; It doesn't matter who or what you desire Me to be; and it doesn't matter what your feelings towards Me are or whether you feel like worshiping or acknowledging Me or not. I AM. Regardless of what you think or feel, I am absolute and nothing or no one can change that."

God wants Moses, and us, to understand that His name is tied to His character, to His being. This is who He is and He will never change. All the outside influences, the circumstances, feelings and desires that weaken our resolve and change us, have no bearing on Him. He knows all, He foresees all, and He has no weakness. He doesn't change.

I, YAHWEH, do not change.
Malachi 3:6 NIV

I CAN BE TRUSTED

Secondly, we see that God, in stating His name, reminds the Israelites that He is the God of their forefathers, Abraham, Isaac and Jacob and therefore He can be trusted. God is telling His people that He will be faithful to them in the same way He was faithful to their ancestors. He is telling them that He will be with them in the same way He was with their ancestors. And He is telling them that He sees them and hears them in the same way he saw and heard their ancestors. He will answer. They only need to trust Him and wait.

Your kingdom is an everlasting kingdom, and Your dominion endures through all generations. The LORD is faithful to all his promises and loving toward all he has made.
Psalm 145:13 NIV

I REMEMBER

Thirdly, God reminds His people that He is the God of the Covenant. He remembers the covenant promise He made to Abraham. "I will make you very fruitful; I will make nations of you, and kings will come from you. I will establish my covenant as an everlasting covenant between Me and you and your descendants after you for the generations to come, to be your God and the God of your descendants after you. The whole land of Canaan, where you now reside as a foreigner, I will give you as an everlasting possession to you and your descendants after you; and I will be their God." (Genesis 17:6-8 NIV)

The Israelites, living as slaves in Egypt for hundreds of years, may have thought God had forgotten them - that He had forgotten the promise He made to His people. But here in Exodus 3, God reminds Moses and His people that He remembers. Again, He reminds them to trust Him and wait.

APPLICATION

The very essence of God's name proclaims that He is unchanging, trustworthy and faithful. In light of this, what are the implications for us?

If God exists as He says and no one or no thing can change His being, then it is important for us to truly know Him. His character, His power, His authority, His commands. Who He is. God reveals Himself through Scripture. We must start there. And as we get to know His character, we begin to align our lives to His truth. We start living out what we believe instead of letting our lives be shaped by how we feel in the moment, or what we desire to be true. We live as Abraham, Isaac and Jacob did - by faith and not by sight. In truth rather than in a lesser version of it. If we are going to live in a manner pleasing and honouring to God, our lives must reflect His unchanging character. And to do this we must know Him in all His fullness. We must believe all that He reveals of Himself to be true.

God wants us to know and trust His faithfulness. He wants us to know that He sees us and hears us. And He wants us to know that He will answer. We, like the Israelites, need only to trust Him and wait in confident expectation.

REFLECTION

Do you know the fullness of His character? What evidence is there in the way you live that God exists? Does your life reflect the truth of who He is?

Psalm 29: Listening Guide

Call to Worship:

1. Psalm 29:1-2: _____ to the LORD.

2. Glory is _____ to God.

3. Child-like faith rests in _____ and _____ .

Motivation to Worship:

4. Psalm 29:3-9: The _____ of the LORD.

5. For God to _____ is for God to _____.

God said . . . and it was so.

God's every Word accomplishes and succeeds in its purposes.

Isaiah 55:10-11

View this teaching session at www.unshakenministries.com

6. Psalm 29 shows us the magnificent _____ of God.

7. Psalm 29 shows us not just the _____ of God, but the _____ of God.

8. The King riding on His chariots of cloud to bring the _____, is symbolic of the King coming to _____!

The One Who is Worshiped:

9. Psalm 29:10-11 The _____; King enthroned.

10. God's power is _____, God's love is _____!

11. John 1:1-3, 14 Jesus: Word made flesh. The _____ and _____ of God come down to dwell among us.

View this teaching session at www.unshakenministries.com

Week Four: God is Good

I have a confession to make. I do not like working out. At all. I know it is good for me and so I force myself to do it with some regularity, but I don't enjoy it. And I don't do it in community, because I am a terrible person while I'm doing it. I mutter awful things about the leader under my breath. With every perky, "Isn't this fun? . . . You go girls, you're rocking this! . . . Doesn't this feel good?" I have a far less cute response. I don't trust the leader because how can I trust someone who is cheerfully shouting lies at me?!

My response to working out reveals my rebellious heart. I want what I want and not what someone tells me I should want. And what I really want, is for what I want to be what I'm allowed to want and encouraged to want. (Could you follow that?)

We know God is who we *should* want. Do we want to want Him? Our journey this week takes us along this path.

---

a WORD to the wise

In this you greatly rejoice, though now for a little while

you may have had to suffer grief in all kinds of trials.

These have come so that your faith – of greater worth than gold,

which perishes though refined by fire – may be proved genuine

and may result in praise, glory and honor when Jesus Christ is revealed.

1 Peter 1:6-7 NIV

Day One: Taste and See (Psalm 34)

Eating is something we do on a daily basis because we need to. Honestly though, when we live in a society where food is plentiful, our reasons for eating often go beyond need. We eat because it brings us pleasure, it brings us together, and it brings us back – the sense of taste is a powerful tool when it comes to memory.

Our sense of taste is sharpest at birth and naturally declines as we age, but beyond the dullness that comes with age, there are actual taste disorders which can create serious health issues. Our sense of taste is an important early warning system which allows us to detect spoiled or harmful ingredients. Loss of taste can lead to potentially dangerous habits like adding too much sugar or salt to food to compensate, or eating too much or too little because no real satisfaction is received. Loss of taste can even lead to depression.[4]

---

[4] Nidcd.nih.gov, http://www.nidcd.nih.gov/health/taste-disorders, last updated January 5, 2014

The title of our Psalm today asks us to taste and see that the LORD is good. It doesn't say, hey, if you're into sweet, you'll like Him. If a salty treat is what you crave, He's your guy. It just says, taste and see. He is good, no matter your taste preferences.

We will be coming at our psalm today through the backdoor, metaphorically speaking.

 1. Based on what you read above regarding taste disorders, what dangers lurk with a spiritual taste disorder?

2. Read through Psalm 34.

The psalm begins with exuberant declarations of praise and invitations for the reader to join in the praise. Then in verse 11 the tone changes. It's sort of like a charismatic speaker jumping all over the stage enthusiastically, before grabbing the mic, narrowing his eyes, and saying, 'Now listen up. Everything is riding on this. I will teach you the fear of the LORD.'

 3. Verse 12 is a rhetorical question – put it in your own words.

4. In response to the rhetorical question raised in verse 12, what does David say should be done in verses 13-14?

5. Verse 15 and 16 raise a sobering contrast – what is it?

 6. This contrast is repeated for emphasis in verses 19 -21 and it is also expanded for greater understanding. What is being contrasted in these verses?

There are echoes of Psalm 1 all over Psalm 34:11-22 because they are both of the wisdom genre. The wisdom genre shows us that there are two ways, two paths with two very different destinations.

Psalm 34:16 tells us the face of the LORD is against those who do evil. Martin Luther writes, "This is a terrible word. If we believed it to be true . . . who would doubt that we would go about far more carefully?"[5]

We assume far too quickly that those the Psalms refer to as wicked or evil are people doing terrible things - the big things like murder. This is not the case at all. We saw in Psalm 1 that the righteous are those who delight in the Lord and His instruction. Who are planted in streams of living water. People who do not have a taste disorder and who crave Him. The word of

---

[5] Luther, from *First Lectures*, 1:161, as quoted by John Goldingay, in *Baker Commentary on the Old Testament: Psalms 1-41* (Baker Academic, Grand Rapids, Michigan, 2006), 484.

warning that is implicit in Psalm 34 is that if you do not crave the taste of God, you are headed for serious trouble. Your taste disorder should trigger a warning.

7. Read Psalm 34:18: Who do you think the crushed in spirit, the broken-hearted people are? (Read Psalm 51:16-17 for further understanding.)

Is your heart broken over sin? Do you mourn over misplaced tastes and cravings?

If so, that is a good place to be. God has a word for people like this.

 8. Read Isaiah 61:1-3 and then turn to Luke 4:16-21. What is God saying to the broken-hearted and crushed in spirit?

9. The final verse of Psalm 34 is a definitive conclusion. What two statements are made?

The word 'redeem' comes from the Latin word 'redimere' which means to buy back. The word condemned comes from the same verb that is used in the first phrase of Psalm 5:10 – "*Make them bear their guilt.*"

 10. With an expanded understanding of these two terms, re-write Psalm 34:22 in your own words.

11. Write down Romans 8:1.

12. Do you live with this reality in mind?

My friends, this is the ultimate goodness of the Lord that we are invited to taste. He bought us back by paying the penalty we owed for sin. We who take refuge in Him do not bear our guilt.

But may all who seek you rejoice and be glad in you;
may those who love your salvation say continually, "Great is the LORD!"
Psalm 40:16 ESV

Talking to God:
Read Psalm 34:1-9 and turn it back to God in prayer.

Day Two: Delight Yourself in the LORD (Psalm 37)

In our journey through the Psalms we have not spent much time looking at context. When studying the Bible, we need to be aware of the elements of context: who did God choose to reveal a particular message to and what are the particulars of the place, time, and people receiving the original words. We also need to be aware of the style a particular passage of Scripture is written in. When we read a verse like one that appears in our psalm today, "The wicked draw the sword and bend their bows to bring down the poor and needy, to slay those whose way is upright; their sword shall enter their own heart, and their bows shall be broken." (Ps 37:14) and correctly read it as poetry, we realize this is not a statement of fact, it is symbolic, a metaphor, a picture intended to reveal a deeper truth.

The book of Psalms is unique in that much of the context surrounding it is ambiguous. Intentionally so. The words of the Psalms are cries of the heart that resonate with people in any time and in many different situations. For that reason, we have not spent a great deal of time establishing contextual links at the beginning of each psalm of study.

Today's psalm is a little different. We have travelled through a number of psalms in the last few weeks and have come across many psalms (in fact most) where rather than encountering the wicked being blown away like chaff and the righteous flourishing like fruitful trees as per the pattern set out in Psalm 1, we have instead seen the wicked prospering and the righteous threatened.

What do we do when what ought to be, is not what is?

We adjust our perspective. The word perspective comes from the Latin word 'per' meaning through and 'specere' meaning to look. We take careful stock of what lens we are looking through.

By the time we get to Psalm 37, we are one quarter of the way through the Psalter. This is the point we encounter a psalm that affirms the perspective of Psalm 1.

Psalm 37 is a reminder: don't let experience overwhelm conviction.

Psalm 37 is a decision to trust even when the evidence does not back up your decision. It is a choice to deliberately shift focus from what is seen, to the One who is not.

> **So we do not lose heart. Though our outer self is wasting away, our inner self is being renewed day by day. For this light momentary affliction is preparing for us an eternal weight of glory beyond all comparison, as we look not to the things that are seen but to the things that are unseen. For the things that are seen are transient, but the things that are unseen are eternal . . . For we walk by faith, not by sight.**
>
> **2 Corinthians 4:16-18, 5:7 ESV**

Walking by faith is hard. It is a conscious, daily, maybe even hourly decision, to say, though I see this with my eyes, I know this with my heart.

1. Read through Psalm 37 and fill in the chart below, doing your best to put the poetical language into your own words.

MY EYES SEE THIS:	MY HEART WILL BELIEVE THIS:
V.1	v.2
V.8	v. 9
V. 12	v.13
V.14	v.15
V.16	v. 17
V.24	v.24
V.32	v.33
V.35	v.36

You might have noticed a phrase that was repeated three times in the first seven verses: fret not.

Fretting messes with our focus and perspective.

2. Verse 10 introduces the word 'wicked' for the first time in this Psalm.
   a. How many times is the word repeated after verse 10?

   b. Why does an author repeat a word or phrase?

The word wicked can also mean 'faithless.'

Hebrews 11 is often referred to as the faith hall of fame. The last verse of Hebrews 10 says that, *"We are not of those who shrink back and are destroyed, but of those who have faith and preserve their souls."* Chapter 11 then opens by telling us what faith is.

 3. Write down the definition of faith according to Hebrews 11:1

 4. How does walking by faith, believing with your heart instead of your eyes, offer peace?

If you were to read the entire chapter you'd see a list of people who were commended for their faith. The list includes many different people, from different times and different situations but you will find one commonality unites them. Not one of them made it into this chapter for the *initial step of faith* required to enter into relationship with God.

Instead, every person in Hebrews 11 is commended for *ongoing acts of believing* at times when their physical eyes could not see what God told them they could believe.

The people of Hebrews 11 were living with laser sharp focus and eternal perspective because their lives depended on it.

Talking to God:

As you talk to God today, discuss your perspective and focus. Ask God to clear your vision and grow your faith as you look beyond what is seen. Pray that God will help you to trust Him, to commit your ways to Him, and to be still before Him, knowing that nothing is impossible with God. Ask God to reveal areas where you lack faith and thank Him that He is faithful.

Day Three: The Meek (Psalm 37)

We are right back in Psalm 37 today. Yesterday we discussed perspective and saw in the Psalm a conscious choice to believe one thing even when our eyes saw another.

1. Read Psalm 37 again today taking special note of verse 11. You may recognize that Jesus quotes Psalm 37:11 in Matthew 5:5 in the Sermon on the Mount. In what two ways are the people who will inherit the land described in verses 9 & 11?

2. Flip to Matthew 5:5 and see Jesus' use of Psalm 37:11. How does Jesus describe the meek?

Both verses carry the loaded term 'meek.' Let's look at it a little more closely, what does the word meek really mean? Now would be a great time to turn to a dictionary and look up the definition and ponder what you find there. But let me caution you, if the dictionary points you in the direction of weak, it's misguided. Meek does not mean weak.

The Bible sees the meek as those who are willing to wait for God.

The meek see things from His perspective, so rather than push their own agendas, they trust that God is working His.

You probably don't need me to tell you that the waiting is hard. We often push ahead instead of choosing to trust, seeking immediate gratification and satisfaction. But that is not God's way.

Be still before the LORD and wait patiently for Him.

Psalm 37:7a ESV

James is a New Testament book that is also part of the wisdom genre. The author is the brother of Jesus, and we will be turning to an interesting passage where we see meekness associated with wisdom and patience associated with perspective.

3. Read James 3:13-4:4.

    a. According to James 3:13, how do we show wisdom and understanding?

    b. According to James 3:14, what two things fight against the meekness of wisdom?

    c. According to James 3:15, where does true wisdom come from?

    d. How is wisdom from above characterised? (verse 17)

    e. What does wisdom from heaven produce? (verse 18)

    f. According James 4:1-4, how is desire connected to all of this?

Much of our inability to wait is related to misplaced desire. We get distracted wanting the wrong things and working hard to get them. We start to fret when we don't have what we want, and we envy when others do.

4. Flip back a few pages to read James 1:16-17. Why do you think these verses start with, 'Do not be deceived . . . ?"

5. Read Psalm 37:4: What does this verse say about desire?

Can we trust God to give us what we really want?

What we desire colours our perspective. In light of that, the order of Psalm 37:4 is interesting. First you delight yourself in the Lord. Then He will give you the desires of your heart.

We need the right perspective before we can appreciate the gifts or the Giver.

6. In what ways have you seen God change the desires of your heart to align with His?

7. Is there something in your life you are struggling to appreciate? How might choosing to see from God's perspective change this?

When you don't have what you want, ask God to work on your wants. When you can't do what you want, ask God to show you what you should do instead. When you face deep hurt and trouble, when you've been wronged, when you've exhausted yourself doing good only to see the wicked prosper, read Psalm 37:28 and know that God will put things right. In doing this, you will learn to wait on God; to submit your agenda to His. You will grow to be one of the meek.

Psalm 37 is a strategically placed reminder not to trust what we see but to live looking through the lens of eternity. We walk by faith and not by sight.

While on earth, we look through the glasses of heaven because we need assistance to focus. But when we get to heaven, our vision will be laser sharp. We will see Him face to face and the things of earth will have passed away along with any desire for them.

Do not love the world or the things in the world. If anyone loves the world, the love of the Father is not in him. For all that is in the world – the desires of the flesh and the desires of the eyes and the pride in possessions – is not from the Father but is from the world. And the world is passing away along with its desires, but whoever does the will of God abides forever.

1 John 2:15-17 ESV

Psalm 37 echoes the themes of Psalm 1 as an encouragement to strengthen our resolve. Of Psalm 37 Martin Luther said, "Oh, such shameful disloyalty, mistrust, and damnable unbelief! We refuse to believe these rich, powerful, and comforting promises of God. When we hear a few threatening words from the wicked, we begin to tremble at the slightest threat. May God help us to obtain the true faith which we see the Scriptures demanding everywhere!"[6]

Amen. May it be so.

Talking to God:

O for a faith that will not shrink, though pressed by many a foe,

That will not tremble on the brink of any earthly woe

That will not murmur or complain beneath the chastening rod,

But in the hour of grief or pain will lean upon its God.

A faith that shines more bright and clear when tempests rage without;

That when in danger knows no fear, in darkness feels no doubt!

Lord, give us such a faith as this; and then, whate'er may come,

We'll taste e'en here the hallowed bliss of an eternal home.

William H. Bathurst, 1796-1877

Day Four: The Measure of My Days (Psalm 39)

We've been taking a hard look at our wants this week. As sinful people struggling with misplaced tastes and desires, we are being confronted with learning to want what is best for us. Today we are going to shift our focus slightly and look more closely at the why's behind the wants. Today we face some of life's big questions. Questions we have, but perhaps feel scared to voice. Questions that echo, but maybe don't feel safe to repeat. Difficult questions that will require us to wrestle. With life. With God.

1. Begin by reading Psalm 39.
    a. What does David say he will do in verse 1?

    b. What happened when he stayed silent? (verses 2-3)

    c. What are the issues David is struggling with in this Psalm? What can't he keep silent about? (verses 4-11)

---

[6] Luther, *Selected Psalms*, 3:229, quoted by John Goldingay, in *Baker Commentary on the Old Testament: Wisdom and Psalms, Psalm 1-41* (Baker Academic, Grand Rapids, Michigan, 2006) 535.

    d.   According to David, what is God doing in verses 9-11?

    e.   What evidence is there that David is struggling to see things from God's perspective?

David is trying to see things from God's perspective. In verse 4 he asks God to show him and to teach him. In verses 5 and 6 he acknowledges to God, this is how my life looks from your perspective. But David can't help his human vision, and looking through his eyes he can't understand what he sees and what he feels.

David is not struggling with small or insignificant issues. These are the big life questions: Why are we here? What is the point of life? Why is it so short? Why is God's presence, His hand, His intervention, a source of pain?

Does it sometimes look easier to reconcile the big questions without God? Does pointlessness seem easier to reconcile if we leave God out of the picture?

The conclusion of Psalm 39 shows us that David is bothered by the heavy-handed harshness of God. If we are vulnerable, no more than a breath and a shadow, why would God deal so severely with us? The question burned and David says, "I tried to keep silent but I couldn't."

Psalms such as this one are included in God's Word. Books like Ecclesiastes, characterised by the key-word vanity, a book which audibly struggles through the big questions, are included in God's Word. The Bible tells the story of Job and does not leave out the part where he hits his breaking point. He suffered greatly, warned his wife about voicing her feelings in a rash manner lest she sin (Job 2:10), kept silent for a week (Job 2:13-3:1) and then lost it and opened his mouth to curse the day of his birth (Job 2:13-3:1). It's all in the Bible. Why?!

2. Turn to Job 7. Job says I'm dying anyway, why stay silent? He turns his voice to God in verse 12. Read Job 7:12-21.

    a.   What does he accuse God of doing in verses 13-14?

    b.   What does he ask God to do in verse 16?

    c.   What question do verses 17-18 bring before God?

    d.   Put verse 20 in your own words.

   e.   Can you relate to how Job is feeling? Explain.

Job is not treading delicately where God is concerned. David did not tread lightly where God was concerned. Both David and Job are bothered by the paradox of why God deals so harshly with frail and fleeting humanity.

   3.   "Everything difficult indicates something more than our theory of life yet embraces."[7] How do you think this quote is relevant to what we've been studying?

We live in a noisy time of quick but shallow answers. Many of us have not learned how to sit with our questions in silence and bring them to God. We turn to Google for answers. We find a relevant podcast that will answer questions and tie up lose ends. Maybe, in our distracted busyness, we don't even ask good questions.

   4.   What questions are you are wrestling with before God?

The decision to leave today with questions and little in the way of answers is intentional. We will come back to Psalm 39 tomorrow. Today, we wrestle with God in the dark.

Talking to God:

Write your own psalm to God today. Ask Him to help you see things from His perspective. As you struggle to understand His ways and wrestle with the tough questions, ask for your eyes to be opened to the work He is doing in, and through, and around you. See if you can bring your psalm around to end on a note of confidence. He is working and even when you don't know the why, you can know the Who.

But blessed are your eyes because they see.

Matthew 13:16a ESV

---

[7] *George MacDonald: an Anthology*, ed. C.S. Lewis (Bles, 1946), para. 85, p. 49. As quoted by Derek Kidner, in *Kidner Classic Commentaries, Psalms 1-72* (InterVarsity Press, 1973) 175.

Day Five: I am a Sojourner (Psalm 39)

But God said to him,

"Fool! This night your soul is required of you, and the things you have prepared,

whose will they be?"

Luke 12:20 ESV

In our homework yesterday, we struggled alongside David and Job with difficult questions. We wondered if there was a purpose to the heavy hand of God on frail and fleeting humanity. Today we lean harder into the why.

  1. Begin by reading Psalm 39.

      a. What does David remind God that he is in verse 12?

      b. Why is it important that David knew he was a stranger and alien in this life?

David knows Scripture. By referring to himself as a sojourner, David is reminding God of the rules He gave to his people as they entered the Promised Land.

2. Read Leviticus 25:23-24: Who owns the land and how does that affect land transactions?

      a. According to verse 24, what must be provided for?

    b. What do you think was the point of this law?

    c. How do you think having a safe-guard like this impacted perspective?

God was reinforcing to His people that they did not own the land; He did. His purpose was not to keep the land *from* His people, but to safeguard it *for* them. God's law established avenues of redemption for people who ran into difficulty, it protected against permanent loss, and it set forth a way and time for return. His people could be confident in the security of their inheritance, and thus be good stewards of it.

  3. What does Psalm 39:11 say God is doing? (See NLT for further clarity)

---

4. How does what you learned about safe-guards in Leviticus 25:23-24, deepen your understanding of what God is doing here?

Beloved, I urge you as sojourners and exiles to abstain from the passions of the flesh which wage war against your soul.

1 Peter 2:11 ESV

The safeguards God wants us to place around our desires is for the protection of our very souls.

The reason God goes after our wants is not because He is trying to *keep stuff from* us, He is *safeguarding the real treasure for* us.

As we struggle to uncover and release our desires to God, as we learn to walk in trust on wobbly legs that grow stronger with use, we will keep bumping into the idea of perspective. Without sound vision we won't see clearly enough to walk well.

People who are near-sighted can clearly see objects that are close up, however, they struggle to focus on that which is distant. People who struggle with far-sightedness can see objects that are faraway clearly, but objects that are right in front of them are blurry.

Neither extreme is good and each has its consequences.

5. From a spiritual perspective, what are the dangers associated with near-sightedness and with far-sightedness?

    a. What benefits come with having objects in the distance in clear focus, and with having objects close up in focus?

    b. How is your vision? Are you spiritually near-sighted or far-sighted? Explain.

The struggle of yesterday is answered today, but we have come at in a round-a-bout manner. The authors of Job, Psalms, and Ecclesiastes did not yet have the prescription they needed to view the big questions with focus. Not because they weren't men of great faith. hey were. It's because the prescription they needed had not yet been made available.

The prescription they needed was Jesus.

> These were all commended for their faith, yet none of them received what had been
> promised. God had planned something better for us so that only together with us would they
> be made perfect.

Hebrews 11:39-40 NIV

In the verses immediately following Hebrews 11:39-40 above, the author of Hebrews says, run
well, you are running together with a great cloud of witnesses. And then it says - what?!

 6.   Read Hebrews 12:3-7: What is this saying?!

We are disciplined so we can share in His holiness. We are made to endure because we are
being prepared for eternity; refined for treasure that will last. God's discipline of us reveals Him
as a good and loving Father who wants the best for us.

The dark confusion of David and Job yesterday was that God had made their hearts for eternity,
but their bodies weren't experiencing it. There was a disconnect between how they were created
to be, and how life was actually playing out.

The only answer to the disconnect is Jesus.

Apart from Christ, the discipline of God as a father is painful and pointless. In Christ, it is the
refining process for our inheritance which is far grander than the moth-eaten treasures of earth.
God our Father is safeguarding our eternal, imperishable inheritance by going after what we
want and why we want it.

> **Blessed be the God and Father of our Lord Jesus Christ! According to his great mercy,
> he has caused us to be born again to a living hope through the resurrection of Jesus
> Christ from the dead, to an inheritance that is imperishable, undefiled, and unfading,
> kept in heaven for you, who by God's power are being guarded through faith for a
> salvation ready to be revealed in the last time. In this you rejoice, though now for a
> little while, if necessary, you have been grieved by various trials, so that the tested
> genuineness of your faith – more precious than gold that perishes though it is tested
> by fire – may be found to result in praise and glory and honour at the revelation of
> Jesus Christ.**
> **1 Peter 1:3-7 ESV**

> *"The only way to the resurrection is via Gethsemane; Psalm 39 is a prayer Jesus might have
> prayed there, and one that believers on the way to resurrection still pray."[8]*

---

[8] Goldingay, 565.

Talking to God:

O child of God, wait patiently when dark thy path may be,

And let thy faith lean trustingly on Him who cares for thee.

And though the clouds hang drearily upon the brow of night,

Yet in the morning joy will come, and fill thy soul with light!

O child of God He loveth thee and thou art all His own;

With gentle hand He leadeth thee, thou dost not walk alone;

And though thou watchest wearily the long and stormy night,

Yet in the morning joy will come, and fill thy soul with light!

O child of God, how peacefully He calms thy fears to rest,

And draws thee upward tenderly, where dwell the pure and blest;

And he who bendeth silently above the gloom of night,

Will take thee home where endless joy shall fill thy soul with light!

Fanny J. Crosby, 1820-1915

DIGGING DEEPER: The Fear of the Lord

Fear. We've known it all our lives. We do our best to avoid it. The knot in the pit of our stomach. Our racing heart. Clammy palms. Sometimes it's more a feeling of dread. Other times it's downright terror. Either way, it's not pleasant and so our experiences often lead us to a negative view of fear.

Even the dictionary definition of fear points us in this direction. It defines fear as "an unpleasant emotion caused by the belief that someone or something is dangerous, likely to cause pain, or a threat."

The fear of the LORD is his treasure. Isaiah 33:6 ESV
He will delight in the fear of the LORD. Isaiah 11:3 NIV
Serve the Lord with fear and rejoice with trembling. Psalms 2:11 ESV

What do we do with verses like these? How do we reconcile them with our experience and understanding of fear? First, we must distinguish between our definition of fear and the Bible's definition. What does the Bible mean when it says we must fear the Lord? According to Reference.com, fearing the Lord means to have reverence and respect for God and His teachings. It refers to a positive Christian attitude that results in obedience and a healthy fear of the consequences for disobeying God's word.

From this definition, we see that fearing God comes from an attitude of love, awe, and respect for God which leads to a strong desire to please Him. We want to obey Him. We choose to obey Him. We know the consequences if we don't. Punishment doesn't drive this fear, rather it is driven by a genuine love for God our Father. It's the fear of displeasing or offending the One on whom our affections are directed.

What does a healthy fear of God look like? Let's look at what Scripture has to say:

It is a dreadful thing to fall into the hands of the living God.
Hebrews 10:31 NIV
My name is to be feared among the nations.
Malachi 1:14 NIV
I tell you, my friends, do not be afraid of those who kill the body and after that can do no more. But I will show you whom you should fear: Fear him who, after the killing of your body, has power to throw you into hell. Yes, I tell you, fear him.
Luke 12:4-5 NIV

Passages like these put fear in our hearts. They give us two separate and distinct images of God: God who judges and punishes, and Jesus, the God who loves us unconditionally. We then tend to associate with one image over another. We're okay with the God of love, but not the God who judges and disciplines. We make God into someone we are more comfortable with. We want to think that our God of love simply overlooks our sinful behaviour and won't judge us for it. But that is not our God.

Note then the kindness and the severity of God: severity toward those who have fallen, but God's kindness to you, provided you continue in his kindness. Otherwise you too will be cut off. Romans 11:22 ESV

To properly understand what it means to fear God, we must see God in His fullness as both a God of love and a God of wrath who punishes His children because of His great love for them.

But because of your hard and impenitent heart you are storing up wrath for yourself on the day of wrath when God's righteous judgment will be revealed.
Romans 2:5ESV

Since we have now been justified by His blood, how much more shall we be saved from God's wrath through [Jesus Christ].
Romans 5:9 NIV

Scripture reveals both aspects of God's character: His love and His wrath. We who are sure of our salvation don't need to live in fear of His punishment for we are saved through grace. But we must know this God, all aspects of His character. We need to be aware of the consequences of living outside of His will. We need to know the parameters He places on us. And then we will experience His love with a holy fear. Trembling at the power and might of this God who holds all of eternity in His hand.

There are several components to the fear of God which we'll look at in greater detail: reverence and awe of God, love and trust in God, obedience and right living, and a humble and repentant heart.

Reverence & Awe

The dictionary defines awe as "a feeling of reverential respect mixed with fear or wonder." Reverence is defined as, "deep respect for someone or something." In Biblical fear, our awe and reverence is directed towards God alone.

Yours, O LORD, is the greatness and the power and the glory and the victory and the majesty,
For all that is in the heavens and in the earth is yours. Yours is the kingdom, O LORD, and you are exalted as head above all.
1 Chronicles 29:11 ESV

In the fear of the Lord, there is an understanding of who God is and an awareness of His unquestionable power and the amazing works of His hand. We see all that He is capable of and stand in awe because of His great awesomeness.

Love & Trust

You who fear the LORD, trust in the LORD; He is their help and their shield.
Psalm 115:11 ESV

As we come to understand this reverential fear of God our knowledge of who He is expands and our love and trust in Him grows. But how can we love what we fear? Again, we need to recognize what a healthy fear of God looks like.

There is no fear in love. But perfect love drives out fear, because fear has to do with punishment. The one who fears is not made perfect in love.
1 John 4:18 NIV

John is saying when we have a right relationship with God, when we trust Him, when we walk in His ways, when we experience His genuine love for us, we don't need to fear His judgment because we are confident in our salvation.

So how does this trust, this loving relationship lead to a fear of God? And how does a healthy fear of God increase our love and trust in Him?

As we spend time with God in prayer and in His Word, we come to know Him; His character, His love and even His righteous anger. We see His amazing grace and His many blessings. And we see His mercy. His Faithfulness. He is true to His promises and we can confidently put our trust in Him. Even when we can't see. Even when the valley is dark. Even when hope seems lost. We can trust His love. We can trust that He is working. We can trust that He is faithful. When we trust His character and trust His Word despite what we see, that's faith. When we fix our eyes on God instead of the storm and allow truth to influence our feelings and emotions instead of circumstances, that's faith. We are called by God to live by faith and not by sight. Our faith grows as our love and trust in God grows and as we grow in our faith we grow in the knowledge of the fear of the Lord.

Trust in the LORD with all your heart, and do not lean on your own understanding.
In all your ways acknowledge him, and he will make straight your paths.
Proverbs 3:5-6 ESV

Obedience & Right Living

Knowing God has every right to judge us harshly, knowing He alone controls our destiny, and knowing He alone has power over death, should put the fear of God into us. It should ignite within us a desire to please Him instead of the world and to live for Him instead of ourselves. We should be afraid of living outside His will.

But knowing He offers us mercy instead of judgment, acceptance instead of shame and life instead of death should fill us with awe and gratitude at His grace and motivate our obedience to Him.

How blessed is everyone who fears the LORD, who walks in His ways.
Psalm 128:1 ESV
Do not be afraid. God has come to test you, so that the fear of God will be with you to keep you from sinning.
Exodus 20:20 NIV
Blessed is the man . . . [who delights] in the law of the LORD, and on His law he meditates day and night.
Psalm 1:2 ESV

The fear of God leads to right living. Right living comes from a knowledge of God and His Word. From delighting in His ways.

We learned in our homework in week one that those who delight in God's law, His commands, are the righteous ones. Those who choose to walk in His ways. Those who choose to love God with all their heart, soul, mind and strength. As we learn to fear God and grow in wisdom and understanding of who He is and all He has done for us we come to find joy in God's ways and in His commands. We enjoy spending time in His Word and in His company and we come to seek Him first. His leading, His guiding, His truth and His way.

Humility & Repentance

The reward for humility and fear of the LORD is riches and honour and life.
Proverbs 22:4 ESV
Blessed is the man who always fears the LORD, but he who hardens his heart falls into trouble.
Proverbs 28:14 NIV
This is the one I esteem: he who is humble and contrite in spirit, and trembles at my word.
Isaiah 66:2 NIV

This is the blessing of a proper fear of the Lord: it produces a humble and repentant heart. Those who are humble, who recognize their absolute and complete dependence on God in all things, and who are contrite in spirit, who grieve their sin and desire to live in a manner pleasing to God, are the ones God blesses. As we recognize God's authority in our lives and know without a shadow of a doubt His power and might, our hearts are softened towards Him. We see how little we are compared to Him and we are humbled because of it.

When I consider Your heavens, the work of Your fingers, the moon and the stars, which You have set in place, what is man that You are mindful of him, the son of man that You care for Him?
Psalm 8:3-4 NIV

Tim Keller defined Biblical fear as "wonder-filled bold humility." It is in humility and grace that we come with bold confidence before the throne of the one and only God, Creator of heaven & earth and "wonder how He could love [us, sinners] condemned unclean."

Conclusion

Our God is a God of love, yet we must also remember His wrath.

Therefore, since we are receiving a kingdom that cannot be shaken, let us be thankful, and so worship God acceptably with reverence and awe, for our God is a consuming fire.
Hebrews 12:28 NIV

We need to remember Whose presence we are entering. We cannot approach God with a cavalier spirit. He must be approached with trembling. Not the trembling of someone running from God. But the kind of trembling that reveals our humble and deep love, respect and honour for Him.

As theologian John Piper wrote so beautifully, "God is horrifically dangerous to run away from but when we walk beside Him, His growl is one of protection."[9]

God promises His protection over those who fear Him. Protection from death. Strength for the weary. Refuge for the soul.

God is our refuge and strength, a very present help in trouble. Psalm 46:1 ESV
Like the eagle that stirs up its nest, and hovers over its young, God spreads wings to catch you, and carries you on pinions.
Deuteronomy 32:11-12 NIV

---

[9] http://www.desiringgod.org/interviews/what-does-it-mean-for-the-christian-to-fear-god - John Piper

He is the fortress in whom we trust. Through His Son, Jesus Christ, we have eternal hope, eternal joy, and eternal life. We have a safe place to run.

The angel of the LORD encamps around those who fear Him, and delivers them.
Psalm 34:7 ESV

John Piper tells a beautiful story of the fear of the Lord. Picture yourself standing on a ledge on the side of a mountain. You see a storm approaching on the horizon. Desperately you look for shelter. Finding some, you tuck yourself inside as the storm hits in all its power, wrath, majesty and awe. From inside the crevice you know you are completely safe, so the horrific danger that looms outside is transposed into awe and wonder. From the safety of your hideout you can now enjoy the storm without fearing it.

He goes on to say that this is what the cross is. Jesus died so we could experience a safe place from which to enjoy the majesty of God. A place of trembling at His power and might. A place of trembling in awe. Trembling, but not cowering.[10]

As we come to understand the grace of our Father and our forgiveness through Christ, our fear of the Lord, our awe and wonder of Him increases. As our fear of God increases, our perspective on who God is and who we are in light of Him becomes clearer. We begin to delight in His law, to align our lives to His way, and to pursue His will for our lives. And through His Word, we grow in our understanding of who our God is, His holiness and His grace for us, His children, and we start living for His glory instead of our own.

Fear of the Lord comes from a right understanding of who God is. It comes from humbling ourselves and acknowledging God's ultimate authority in our lives. It comes from awe and respect of God, a proper reverence of Him. And it leads us to a deeper trust and genuine love of our heavenly Father.

> *'Twas grace that taught my heart to fear*
> *And grace my fears relieved.*
> *How precious did that grace appear*
> *The hour I first believed.*
>
> Amazing Grace
> John Newton

How great is Your goodness, which you have stored up for those who fear You, which You bestow in the sight of men on those who take refuge in You.
Psalm 31:19 NIV

---

[10] Ibid.

Psalm 40: Listening Guide

The Rescue (Psalm 40:1-2):

1. I waited patiently, the LORD _____ my cry. (Psalm 40:1)

2. Pits are isolating places where we can lose our _____.

3. Pits don't come with _____.

4. We don't lose heart when we have _____ in the waiting.

5. Sometimes God pulls us _____ of the pit. Sometimes He gives us _____ in it.

6. God _____, and then God _____.

The Report (Psalm 40:3-10):

7. A song of praise to _____!

8. Many will _____. They will _____. They will put their _____ in God.

9. Having experienced the rescue, obedience will become the _____ of our hearts.

View this teaching session at www.unshakenministries.com

The Relapse (Psalm 40:11-15):

10. Oops . . . . I _____ again.

11. There is _____ only one place to run for help!

12. Micah 7:7-9: The issue of your sin is between

_____.

The Response (Psalm 40:16-17):

13. While waiting in the pit again: _____ is the LORD!

Now the salvation and the power and the kingdom of our God and the authority of his Christ have come, for the accuser of our brothers has been thrown down, who accuses them day and night before our God.

And they have conquered him by the blood of the Lamb and the word of their testimony, for they loved not their lives even unto death! (Revelation 12:10-11 ESV)

View this teaching session at www.unshakenministries.com

Week Five: A Refuge for the Broken

"Because I am your parent, and I said so."

It was the answer I hated to hear as a child. I saw the response as an easy out. An excuse. My parents obviously didn't want me to have any fun, but they weren't ready to admit this was the reason for their no.

Yet, for better or worse, it is the answer I as a parent have given to my children. I see the response differently now. There are times I am weary of explaining. I am tired of having to present my case before a very little, and not always very intelligent, jury. There are reasons for my no that are beyond their ability to understand so as the older, wiser, and more experienced party, I pull out the authority trump card.

Why is this even an issue though? Why do my children question my authority as a parent to make this statement in the first place?

Because my beautiful children have rebellious natures. Rebellious natures they have inherited from me. This week we encounter the authoritative character of God. He has all the authority. But there is no safer place for ultimate power to reside than with the One who is Steadfast Love and Abounding Mercy.

Though our sinful nature must be broken, He only breaks to mend. Though He will judge all in righteousness, His judgement puts all back to right.

Powerful God is a refuge for the broken.

---

a WORD to the wise

The LORD will roar from Zion and thunder from Jerusalem;

the earth and sky will tremble.

But the LORD will be a refuge for His people,

a stronghold for the people of Israel.

Joel 3:16 NIV

Day One: Be Still (Psalm 46)

Be still and know that I am God

How many of us have read that verse and pictured a quiet call from a gentle shepherd? He lounges on the thick grass of a sun-soaked meadow, and pats the ground beside him. Beckoning us to lay down, he points up to fluffy clouds drifting across a background of clear blue sky, while lines from Charles Wesley's poem, Gentle Jesus, Meek and Mild are whispered on the wind . . .

I was in the middle of the daunting feat that is getting groceries with four pre-schoolers. My eyes bounced rapidly between grocery list, grocery cart, grocery shelves, and four busy bodies. Suddenly I realized there were only three. I panicked – how many aisles since I'd seen my daughter?!

I did not softly and tenderly call her. I did not stand in the produce section with arms outstretched inviting her to come. I immediately began racing my overflowing cart up and down the aisles, three little boys trailing behind me as I shouted Skye's name. I must have been a terrifying sight as I ran through the store bellowing loudly: come back to me, child.

Fear taught my daughter a valuable lesson that day. She learned she is safest when she stays with me.

I love my children. I spent many nights singing tenderly over them as I rocked them to sleep. When they come running to me with their hurts, I respond with open arms and words of love. I can be tender and soft. A refuge from their fears and hurts.

But when their wanderings are dangerous, the same love which displays itself softly and tenderly will demonstrate itself with firmness and loud displays of power and authority for their own good. Instilling my children with healthy fear is loving as I seek to be a refuge from danger.

We come to Psalm 46 today and as we read it over, many will recognize the familiar call to be still and know He is God. But perhaps we have not realized the context within which this statement is made. Perhaps we have not heard the tone of the command before.

1. Read Psalm 46.
    a. What three things does the author declare that God is in verse one?

    b. What is the result of knowing this? (first four words after 'therefore' in verse 2) (ESV)

    c. Even though . . . what is being described in the rest of verse 2 and 3?

d.   What is being described in verse 4?

e.   What does verse 5 say about this holy city?

f.   Even though . . . what is described in verse 6?

g.   What is being commanded in verse 8?

h.   What is being described in verse 9?

i.   Knowing the context of the entire Psalm, what is the tone of the warning in verse 10?

j.   Verses 7 and 11 are like a refrain. Put them in your own words to help you better understand what they are saying.

The opening stanza (verses 1-3) showcases magnificent personification. We see the sea roaring in rage. It throws itself at the mountains and these monuments of stone tremble and are moved. This is an image of absolute chaos in the natural realm.

The second stanza (verses 4-7) shows nations raging and kingdoms being moved. The voice that spoke all that exists into being, speaks again and this time the earth melts.

The third stanza opens with a command, "Come, behold the works of the LORD, how he has brought desolations on the earth."

God of angel armies has brought an end to war. He has ended it by utterly destroying anything that could be used to make war against Him.

Into that context comes the injunction, "Be still!"

2.   Again, knowing the context of the entire Psalm, how do you better understand verse 10? What is the message?

This is not a gentle invitation! This is an authoritative command into a world of loud chaos. It is a warning to acknowledge who He is and to acknowledge what is His. Verse ten is a firm declaration that the glory is His and His alone and He will fight to defend it.

3. In the midst of the war, what does verse 1 say God is to His people?

 4. In what ways do you see God as a refuge to His people in this Psalm?

5. In what ways has God been a refuge for you?

6. Have you found that in experiencing God as your refuge, you can now honestly exclaim with the psalmist, I will not fear? (verse 2) Explain.

God is our tender Father, but He is also the all-powerful King of Angel Armies who fights to defend His glory. It might seem paradoxical to think of Warrior God as a refuge and fortress. Until you think of the point of a fortress. Fortifications were built to protect people in case of an attack. In times of peace the gates to the fortress would remain open so people could come and go as they pleased. In times of war, people would run to the fortress wanting to be let in, wanting the gates to close behind them to keep them safe from attack. The people put their hope in the fact that their fortress was stronger than their enemy. That their place of refuge was strong enough to keep them safe.

Psalm 46 shows us the chaos, the raging against, the war. Psalm 46 shows us the need for a safe refuge. This psalm echoes a refrain in verse one, seven, and eleven: God is with us; our strong fortress. Psalm 46 shows us that in the conflict we have a safe refuge to run to. Warrior God who defeats all enemies is the fortress.

God is not calling you into *a* fortress, He is calling you into *His* fortress. He *is* the fortress.

> The LORD roars from Zion, and utters his voice from Jerusalem, and the heavens and the earth quake. But the LORD is a refuge to his people, a stronghold to the people of Israel.

Joel 3:16 ESV

 7. Though mountains be moved, though kingdoms be moved, what won't be moved according to Psalm 46:5? Why?

Though all else be moved, His city will not. Though the setting is one of chaos and conflict, God is in the midst of it and He will not be moved. He is a very present help in times of trouble and the reason we need not fear.

The city that won't be moved is an eternal city. Its members are those who reside in Christ. As we close today, see the final vision from Revelation. The eternal city established by and for the glory of God. An everlasting refuge of peace and safety.

Then I saw a new heaven and a new earth, for the first heaven and the first earth had passed away, and *the sea was no more.* **And I saw the holy city, new Jerusalem, coming down out of heaven from God, prepared as a bride adorned for her husband. And I heard a loud voice from the throne saying, "Behold, the dwelling place of God is with man"** . . . **And the city has no need of sun or moon to shine on it, for the glory of God gives it light, and its lamp is the Lamb . . . its gates will never be shut . . .**

Revelation 21:1-3, 23, 25 ESV

Talking to God:

When the disciples faced a great storm, they awoke Jesus by asking, "Do you not care that we are perishing?" Jesus responded by rebuking the wind and the sea saying, "Peace! Be still!" Jesus then asked His disciples, "Why are you so afraid? Have you still no faith?" (Mark 4:38-41 ESV)

The disciples were in the presence of the One true refuge. The only One who could save them from perishing, and they were still afraid. Lean into Jesus today as you come before the Father. Only He can rebuke the chaos that threatens to undo you. Jesus is a safe and secure refuge for the broken.

Day Two: God Himself Is Judge (Psalm 50)

If the voice of God commanded attention yesterday, it thunders today. In the opening lines of Psalm 50, we see the only Psalm addressed to God using three different titles. *The Mighty One* – God above all gods; *God* – God above creation; *the LORD* – God of the covenant. This God is on His throne and He has summoned heaven and earth and all that is in it to come before His presence. Psalm 50 is considered an oracular hymn; a prophetic psalm.

1. Though our focus today will be on the first 15 verses of Psalm 50, read through all of the Psalm.
    a. Who does God summon? (verse 5) Why? (verse 4)

    b. What does God not want and why? (verse 8-11)

c. What does He want instead? (verses 14-15)

God the Mighty King is calling out the people who have entered into covenant with Him. Do you see the repetition in verses 4 and 5? *His people, my faithful ones, who made a covenant with me . . .*

2. What did Peter, a disciple of Jesus, say in 1 Peter 4:17?

3. What is the intended purpose of judgement?

4. Read 1 Peter 1:6-7 – how does this change or reinforce your understanding of the purpose of judgement?

I find this to be a sobering word even as I write it: judgement must begin with those of us who have willingly entered into covenant/relationship with God.

5. Why do you think judgment must begin with those who have willingly entered into relationship with God?

6. How does Matthew 7:5 speak to this?

Psalm 50 is a prophetic psalm of judgment and it is also a covenant psalm. This psalm is chalk full of covenant language and it is beyond exciting. Seriously, stick with me because it was one of the high points of my week when I saw this!

Exodus tells an amazing story that if you had read it first in a fiction novel, your eyes would have bugged out of your head – it is literally best-seller material!!

The chosen people of God were enslaved by the world superpower. They were treated horrifically and were so oppressed they had no means of escape. God enters the picture (well, He was always there, but He speaks into the situation) and says, I see; I hear; I know; I have come down to deliver my people. (Exodus 3:7-8)

Using Moses, God unleashes a series of plagues on the Egyptians to mightily deliver His people. Pharaoh lets God's people go, but then has a change of heart and sends his army after them. God's people are standing at the edge of the sea when they become aware they are being pursued; not a big deal for God. He sends His people across it; they escape on dry land. Their escape leads them into the barrenness of a desert where God feeds them with bread from heaven and birds that fall out of the sky. He quenches their thirst with water gushing from a rock.

Having demonstrated His desire to be in relationship, God now gives Moses the law to show the people how this relationship will work. Moses passes the law on to the people of Israel.

7. As Moses stands before the people, what does he tell them? (Exodus 24:3)

8. What is their response?

9. Moses writes down all the words of the LORD and then gets up early in the morning to build an altar and twelve pillars, one for each tribe of Israel. Then Moses and some chosen people make sacrifices. What does Moses do next and how do the people respond? (Exodus 24:7)

10. Write down Moses' words in Exodus 24:8.

11. Now, prepare to get a little bugged-eyed. What happens next?! Exodus 24:9-11

Moses, Aaron, his sons, and 70 of the elders have just participated in what was called the peace offering. The peace offering was the only kind of sacrifice in which the worshiper ate some of the sacrificial animal.[11] The whole point of this was a shared meal; community. God was the host and those who sacrificed were the welcome guests.

12. Re-read Exodus 24:8 and then turn to Matthew 26:26-28. Write down the words of Jesus in Matthew 26:28.

We who are in Christ have willingly entered into Him through His sacrifice and have been invited to eat in His presence.

 13. Read Hebrews 9:11-14.
    a. What has Jesus secured for us and how did He secure it?

---

[11] *ESV Study Bible Commentary* (Crossay2008), 998.

b. What are we to be purified from? (verse 14)

In Psalm 50 Mighty God upon His throne calls all creation to His judgment seat and He starts with those who have entered into covenant with Him. Sin requires an accounting. But we can rest secure because the death of Jesus accounted for our sin. He washes us clean. In Jesus, God sees us through the filter of the only sacrifice that truly saves – the blood of the perfect Lamb of God.

Talking to God:

If you are a member of the new covenant that Jesus inaugurated with the sacrifice of His own blood, you are being called to examine your heart. Today is not a time to get hung up on actions. Yes, you will account for those, too. However, our actions are an overflow of what is in our hearts. Lay out your motivations and attitudes. Bring your heart to the altar today and let the holy fire of God consume that which left unattended will consume you.

Day Three: God Himself is Judge (Psalm 50)

Day One of this week we heard the command to be still before the LORD God and to acknowledge who He is. We spent yesterday in Psalm 50 and saw that God, Mighty King, comes to judge His people.

1. Begin today by reading through Psalm 50.
    a. Who is God talking to in verse 16?

    b. What does He say to them? (verse 16)

    c. Why does He say these things to them? (verse 17-20)

    d. What very mistaken idea do these people have? (verse 21)

    e. What warning does God speak to these people in verse 22?

    f. What beautiful promise does God give and who is the promise for? (verse 23)

    g. Look back at verse 14, what is the sacrifice that God wants?

h. Had you seen thankfulness as a sacrifice before? Explain.

If you remember from yesterday, God is addressing people who have willingly entered into covenant with Him. Today we see God's response to those who have forgotten the covenant they made. He is coming against them in judgment because they have taken the words of the covenant on their lips but they have not taken them to their hearts.

They have thrown God's words over their shoulders; out of sight out of mind. God's law cannot guide them on their path or convict them of sin because it is not in front of their eyes.

2. Verse 18 carries an indictment of these supposed covenant people – put it into your own words.

3. How do the words of Romans 1:32 and the middle phrase of 1 Timothy 5:22 clarify your understanding?

These faithless people might have thought they were getting away with their disordered hearts. They might have thought that because they were not being 'bad' themselves, they could get away with vicariously enjoying a lifestyle of sin.

> **Because the sentence against an evil deed is not executed speedily, the heart of the children of man is fully set to do evil.**
> **Ecclesiastes 8:11 ESV**

The faithless ones made a grievous misinterpretation of God's silence. So God ended the silence.

Yesterday we read in Exodus about the people of Israel willingly entering into covenant with God. It was a breathtaking ceremony that concluded with a banquet in the very presence of God.

4. Flip back to Exodus 24:9 – who attended this banquet?

Nadab and Abihu, the sons of Aaron, were in the company of men who ate in the presence of God. Let's look at how their story ends in the book of Leviticus. (It's the book immediately following Exodus.) Before we get into the verses we will be looking at, here is a bit of background: Aaron and his sons were consecrated according to the laws God gave. They followed the procedures as God had commanded and presented offerings before God. Leviticus 8:36 says, "Aaron and his sons did all the things that the LORD commanded by Moses."

5. What is the result of them following these commandments according to Leviticus 9:22-24?

6. What happens next? Read Leviticus 10:1-2.

That's a pretty abrupt ending to the story isn't it?! Though Nadab and Abihu had experienced the presence of God, though they had heard the law and completed the rituals, they still didn't get it. Their hearts were still rebellious and they still wanted to do things their own way.

Beware lest there be among you a root bearing poisonous and bitter fruit, one who, when he hears the words of this sworn covenant blesses himself in his heart, saying, 'I shall be safe, though I walk in the stubbornness of my heart.'

Deuteronomy 29:18-19 ESV

Nadab and Abihu learned the terrifying lesson that if you 'forget' God, there will be none left to deliver. You will not be safe.

We cannot walk in the foolishness of our own way and not pay the price.

God has made a way for people to enter into covenant with Him. We are invited to dine in His presence. But to enter the presence of Holy God while harbouring a rebellious heart is a dangerous thing.

We are going to close today with the story of two suppers from chapter 19 in the book of Revelation. The book of Revelation is a series of visions received by the apostle John. This is the vision of two feasts. One of the feasts is called the great supper of God. It begins with John seeing heaven opened to reveal a rider on a white horse. His name is Faithful and True and he is said to judge and make war in righteousness. A sharp sword which he will use to strike down the nations comes from his mouth. (Revelation 19:11-15)

7. Read Revelation 19:17-21: Who is invited to the feast (v17) and who is being feasted on? (18, 21)

Now look back several verses. There is another feast in this same chapter.

8. Read Revelation 19:6-9: Who is attending this feast and what is the occasion?

There is no refuge from the Son, there is only refuge in the Son. You will either attend the feast as the Bride of Christ or you will be the feast. The rider on the white horse is called Faithful and True and He judges rightly. His judgement will make war and will completely destroy anything that could be used to make war against Him.

The warning in Psalm 50:22 is real. So is the promise of Psalm 50:23. Those who order their ways rightly will see the salvation of God.

Faced with our rebellious hearts, the Psalm that follows is a needful one.

Have mercy on me, O God, according to your steadfast love . . . Create in me a clean heart, O God.

Lay your heart out before Holy God today. You can trust that His judgements are right.

Yet the Lord longs to be gracious to You; He rises to show you compassion.

For the Lord is a God of justice. Blessed are all who wait for Him.

Isaiah 30:18 ESV

May we never lose the wonder of His mercy!

Day Four: Create in Me a Clean Heart (Psalm 51)

We are looking more closely at God in His rightful position of authority this week. God has authority over all His creation simply because of who He is. God. The Creator.

God is the judge. We can argue this. We can dilute this. We can ignore this. We have been given the choice to submit to this knowledge or we have been given the freedom to rebel against it for a time. But we don't have the power to change it.

We begin today with the awareness that because God has the authority, He is the judge. The next part is pretty sobering.

God is the judge and we are guilty.

1. Begin today by reading through Psalm 51.
    a. What two requests does David make in verse 1?

    b. What does David acknowledge in verse 3?

    c. Do you live with this same awareness? Explain.

    d. Who does David say he has sinned against in verse 4 and what is the result of that according to the last two lines of the verse?

e. Why is it important that we understand and recognize the truth of verse 4 in our own lives?

f. Put verse 5 in your own words.

Verse 5 isn't merely a casual shoulder shrug that essentially says, yeah I did it but it's not my fault. Verse 5 is a statement of fact.

Who can bring a clean thing out of an unclean? There is not one.

Job 14:4 ESV

What is man, that he can be pure? Or he who is born of a woman, that he can be righteous?

Job 15:14 ESV

2. Summarize Romans 5:12.

We were created in the image of God. When Adam and Eve chose to rebel against their Creator that image was marred. Sin spread to all of us. It is in our nature.

At the time of my writing this, a prominent public figure recently made a comment that he wasn't opposed to asking for forgiveness, he just didn't really think he needed it.

A lot of people will admit they have not followed the Ten Commandments perfectly. But they still feel like they are pretty good people because for the most part they follow the Golden Rule and treat others like they would want to be treated.

3. What does David ask of God in Psalm 51:10?

4. Why might praying that God make this true of you, increase your awareness of sin and your need of repentance?

We're fine thinking of God as love, or God as refuge or protector. We're even okay with thinking of God as a father needing to discipline His children. But when it comes to God as judge, we only want to think about it in terms of Him judging others, not us.

For a judge to be just, offense cannot be overlooked; God is just and He does not overlook sin.

5. Read Psalm 51:1-2 again. On what basis does David make his requests to God? What aspect of God's character is David appealing to?

David recognized his need for cleansing. He knew God was rich in mercy, but payment was still required. David knew this because God had instituted a ceremonial system of sacrifice for His chosen people. God's law required daily sacrifice. Every day His people participated in ritual and ceremony intended to point them to an awareness of the price of sin. Every day they witnessed animals bear the weight of their sin.

I used to think that the priests were the ones sacrificing the animals and the people were somewhat removed from the experience. I was shocked to find out this was not the case.

If his offering is a burnt offering from the herd, he shall offer a male without blemish. He shall bring it to the entrance of the tent of meeting, that he may be accepted before the LORD. He shall lay his hand on the head of the burnt offering, and it shall be accepted for him to make atonement for him.

Leviticus 1:3-4 ESV

When the people were bringing their burnt offerings, their peace offerings, and their sin offerings, they laid their hands on the head of the animal being sacrificed. They were up close and personal with the price of their sin. Death.

The price of sin was death and for a time, the price was paid by animals. But animals couldn't bear the weight of it.

 6. What does Hebrews 10:3-4 say about the Old Testament ceremonial system?

It seems the only way out is a miracle.

Logic dictates that only a Creator can craft a miracle . . .

Tomorrow we will look in depth at the only sacrifice that can truly cleanse. Today, let's rest in the awareness that our hearts need cleansing.

Create in me a clean heart, o God . . .

We are encountering the sureness of our rebellious hearts this week. There is an element of heaviness and pain that comes along with this. But, please don't miss this, there is also wonderful freedom, release, confidence, and joy that comes from bringing our brokenness to the Judge who is also the Creator. Something that is not broken, does not need to be made new. Acknowledging your brokenness to God opens up the space for Him to work. Come before God in confidence today with your brokenness freeing Him to create a new work.

Day Five: Restore to Me the Joy of Salvation (Psalm 51)

I love big, interesting sounding words. The word 'propitiation' ranks right up there with the best of them. To propitiate is to attempt to turn away wrath with an offering.

I have seen this lived out almost daily. My children have attempted to propitiate me with the offer of a bite of their forbidden cookie. I sternly announce it is bedtime. Lights out. No more talking. They call me back to their room and propitiate with just one more hug or kiss.

Yesterday we saw David crying out to God to cleanse his heart. The background of Psalm 51 is given to us for context. David had neglected his duties out of laziness and instead of being on the battlefield with his men, he was in his palace. David lusted after a woman he saw bathing on her rooftop and instead of turning away from temptation, he ordered it brought into his house. When his sin resulted in pregnancy, instead of seeking forgiveness from those he'd offended, David pre-meditated the murder of the man who could expose him. This was no small, isolated whoops. David was in deep.

David was in super-deep before his eyes were opened to the extent of what he'd done. And when his eyes were opened, he didn't run to cover up and hide like Adam and Eve. David ran to God instead of away from Him. Desperate for mercy, David ran to the only judge who could offer him forgiveness and redemption. The only One who could restore the joy of his salvation.

1. Read through Psalm 51: Write down the first line of verse 7.

David is very intentionally using covenant language. In the law that governed daily life for David, anyone who had encountered the dead was considered unclean.

Whoever in the open field touches someone who was killed with a sword or who died naturally, or touches a human bone or a grave, shall be unclean seven days. For the unclean they shall take some ashes of the burnt sin offering, and fresh (living) water shall be added in a vessel. Then a clean person shall take hyssop and dip it in the water and sprinkle it on the tent and on all the furnishings and on the persons who were there and on whoever touched the bone, or the slain or the dead or the grave. And the clean person shall sprinkle it on the unclean on the third day and on the seventh day. Thus on the seventh day he shall

cleanse him, and he shall wash his clothes and bathe himself in water, and at evening he shall be clean.

Numbers 19: 16-19 ESV

2. According to the passage from Numbers above, what two things were put in a vessel for the hyssop to be dipped in and sprinkled on the person who was unclean?

3. What kind of person needed to fulfill this cleansing ritual?

4. Look back at Question 6 from yesterday. What was the ceremonial system unable to do?

5. Read Hebrews 9:19-22. What was the purpose of all the blood in the Old Covenant (the ceremonial system of sacrifice)?

6. What does John the Baptist say when he sees Jesus walking towards him? (John 1:29)

Jesus came as the spotless Lamb of God and He put an end to the ceremonial system of sacrifice because He was the once and for all sacrifice that finally paid the full price of sin.

> **But when Christ had offered for all time a single sacrifice for sins, he sat down at the right hand of God, waiting from that time until his enemies should be made a footstool for his feet. For by a single offering he has perfected for all time those who are being sanctified.**

Hebrews 10:12-14 ESV

This is what's so exciting about this Psalm: even though it lays out the desperation of our situation - we are sinful from birth, we have not just sinned against each other, we have sinned against the One whose image we were made in – even though we have sinned against the Judge who will not overlook sin, we can come to *this very Judge* and request mercy and grace and yes, *justice!*

7. What two things does 1 John 1:9 say God is?

The justice of God is trustworthy because He made a way for the price to be paid. We couldn't pay it ourselves, the animals couldn't bear the weight of our sin, and so God paid the price Himself.

Because Jesus paid the full price of our sins, it would be unjust of God to come after us for payment.

All that ceremonial cleansing with blood was pointing to the One whose blood can really cleanse us, once and for all.

8. In Psalm 51:7 David says, 'wash me, and I will be clean.' What will the result of that cleansing be according to verse 8?

    a. What about according to verse 12?

    b. How about verse 13?

    c. Verse 15?

9. Read Hebrews 9:28: How do you think this verse ties in to what we are looking at?

The end of Psalm 51 is interesting. In verse 16 David says that God does not delight in the sacrifice itself or he would bring it. But then David goes on to say that God will delight in right sacrifices and the sacrifices are offered.

The sacrifices were required. Jesus' ultimate sacrifice was required. But for us to receive the gift of this sacrifice is a heart issue.

A cleansed heart will lead to right behaviour. It will bring a fresh sense of God's presence, a life of integrity that is a living example to the unfaithful, and a joy-filled passion that will naturally share the goodness of God with others.

Psalm 51 is a psalm of confession. But it is also a joy-filled song of restoration. David approaches covenant God, sure of his place within the covenant, sure of the measures that a just God has put in place to deal with covenant-breakers, and confident that his brokenness will lead to dancing.

Talking to God:

Isn't there joy in knowing that God worked His justice to our favour? Isn't there confidence in knowing that because Christ met the legal requirements of the law for us, the price has been paid in full?

Have mercy on me, O God, according to your steadfast love; according to your abundant mercy blot out my transgression. Wash me thoroughly from my iniquity, and cleanse me from my sin!

For I know my transgressions, and my sin is ever before me. Against you, you only have I sinned and done what is evil in your sight, so that you may be justified in your words and blameless in your judgment.

Create in me a clean heart, O God, and renew a right spirit within me. Cast me not away from your presence, and take not your Holy Spirit from me. Restore to me the joy of your salvation, and uphold me with a willing spirit.

Thank God that wherever we see His judgement and wrath rightly falling on the unfaithful, we can know that the possibility for grace and mercy are just around the corner.

CALL TO PRAYER

As a much younger girl, maybe still in junior high, there was the odd time I was required to take the bus home from piano lessons. While I had been taught how to do this task, I was extremely anxious about having to take the bus alone and transfer by myself. When I took the bus with friends, it was a grand adventure and I basically followed my "wiser" friends around.

This was NOT that time. I could feel a pit in the depths of my being. I did fine on the first bus, but I didn't feel fine inside. Trusting that Jesus was with me and cared, I prayed for His peace and protection even as I walked to the next stop. When I got on that second bus and paid my fare, I scanned the rows looking for an empty seat and locked eyes in recognition.

God had placed on that very bus, at that very time, someone who not only knew my name, but one who had lovingly named me; one who knew how to look after me and one who was able to fix all sorts of things. There to take me the rest of the way home was my earthly father. He had left work downtown at exactly the right time to "happen" to connect with me that day. It never happened again.

I remember marveling at the care of my Heavenly Father. God gave me a gift in the reminder that although my dad tenderly loved me, provided me a safe place to live and grow, and even "fixed" many things, he was unable to know all things, or hold all power. While my dad could provide security and safety, he could never be my refuge and fortress. Only God my Father can!

It's in the beholding of God, that we can be held in the goodness and love of His embrace. An embrace gives us comfort, makes us feel safe and protected; cared for. As an embrace holds us, we, in our foolishness can perceive this as limiting, binding, and confining rather than safely holding us back so that we don't rush ahead, straight into danger. How fickle we can be! Forgetting that in these very arms, we have access to the fullest freedoms offered to us - ALL the gifts of the KING of kings!

I sometimes have a hard time being still. It's not that I don't like to be still - I really do; in fact I'm wired that way, I find great joy in sitting in a cozy place preferably with a fluffy blanket, a hot drink, soft lights and a good book, but... Life is busy and with four kids going in different directions, I often feel like I'm a circus ring master coordinating not only the jugglers, but also the hoop spinners, disappearing tricks and a few wild animals. Do you long for stillness too?

There have been a few times in my life where God has imposed stillness upon me and, whilst being inconvenient from an earthly perspective, they brought great eternal blessing into my heart and home. You may not know this about me, because I can hide it well, but sometimes I move too fast and frequently end up breaking things - including myself.

A few Christmas seasons ago, I fell down some stairs at the hockey rink where my son was playing a game and dislocated my shoulder. Entering the holiday season with an immobilized arm and unable to drive was certainly inconvenient, even maddening. But, God... God brought in servers. I had to slow down. I had to be still. I had to receive. My mom rescued me, my husband and kids took on more to help out, friends provided meals and drove around while I listened to and met with God - a refuge for the broken literally and figuratively.

I actively used the time to enter into His presence with thanksgiving. It did indeed feel like a sacrifice to be thankful, and in my own strength it would have been impossible, but His Spirit led the heart yielding. God is NOT impressed in my ability to perform and jump through the hoops and to present the face of perfection. What He is interested in, however, is my broken and contrite spirit, for He is the ONE who will mend it and raise me up with Christ. He desires that I acknowledge Him in the midst of the chaos and that I reorient my disordered heart according to His ways.

My hands have made both heaven and earth; they and everything in them are mine. I, the LORD, have spoken! I will bless those who have humble and contrite hearts, who tremble at my word. But those who choose their own ways- delighting in their detestable sins- will not have their offerings accepted.
Isaiah 66: 2-3a NLT

Submit to God's royal son, or he will become angry, and you will be destroyed in the midst of all your activities - for his anger flares up in an instant. But what joy for all who take refuge in him!
Psalms 2:12 NLT

A disordered heart is the result of our fallen state. The sinful state into which we were born. It has nothing to do with sinning more or less than others and it's not only the things I do that I shouldn't or the things that I leave undone which should be. It is just the state of my being - rebellious, separateness from my Creator because of my very nature (Romans 3:23). But our merciful Father has given a great gift! The blood of His very own Son has cleared us of guilt and we can live open and honest lives, running into the embrace of God, for we have been credited with Christ's own righteousness! (Psalms 32:1-5). We have no fear other than for God Himself and this is the joy of our salvation! Reordered hearts, repentance, restoration, covenant living, relationship with God.

On Our Knees

Pray through the following Scriptures:
Search me, O God, and know my heart; test me and know my anxious thoughts. Point out anything in me that offends you, and lead me along the path of everlasting life.
Psalms 139: 23, 24 NLT

Create in me a clean heart, O God, and renew a right spirit within me.
Psalms 51:10 ESV

Allow yourself to be vulnerable and broken in His presence. For you are safest there - in His refuge. Let Him offer you His embrace as He reveals and convicts. Turn towards Him and allow His forgiveness to overwhelm you. Commit to yield your heart to His. Delight yourself in Him and allow His desires to become your own and live in the overflowing abundance. (Psalms 37:4). The purpose of His conviction is to bring cleansing, healing, restoration and freedom. It is the lie of the enemy that the purpose is your punishment. Restitution has already been paid in Christ! Thank Him for that. Acknowledge that you are a new creation (2 Corinthians 5:17)

Throw off your old sinful nature and your former way of life, which is corrupted by lust and deception. Instead let the Spirit renew your thoughts and attitudes. Put on your new nature, created to be like God - truly righteous and holy.
Ephesians 4:22-24 NLT

May we delight not in ourselves and especially not in our own sin and idolatry, but in You alone. May we not run after counterfeit "quick-fix" distractions, but run to find refuge in YOU alone. Thank you, Lord, for my new heart and my new nature - holy and righteous. No longer sinner, but redeemed saint.
Amen!

Psalm 72: Listening Guide

History is the story of the past. Knowing the story of the past shapes our knowledge of the present, and informs the future.

What Can We Learn From the Past?

1. The image of God as Shepherd reveals His _____ for us.

2. The image of God as King reveals His _____ to us.

3. Pharaoh used his power as king to _____ justice. God uses His power as King to _____ justice.

We only trust a refuge if we believe it to be more powerful than that which we are seeking refuge from.

4. A generation had to be raised up on the daily provision of God before they were ready for their King to lead them into _____ .

5. God was reminding His people of the truth of their _____, to prepare them for the reality of the _____, and train them for the promise of the _____ .

The promise of the future rested on obedience in the present. The motivation for obedience in the present should be God's displays of power in the past.

View this teaching session at www.unshakenministries.com

6. Deuteronomy 17:14-17:
   a. Kings of Israel were not to amass military _____.

   b. Kings of Israel were not to take many _____.

   c. Kings of Israel were not to amass _____.

How Does This Inform Our Present?

7. Deuteronomy 17:18-20: How were the kings of Israel to protect against this? _____ the law down. Keep it _____ them. _____ it daily.

8. We don't want to be _____ from the people around us, even if that is how the blessing of God will be shown to the whole world. We want to _____ the people around us, no matter the cost!

9. What is your heart _____ to? (Deuteronomy 10:20, Deuteronomy 13:4, Deuteronomy 30:20)

What Are the Implications For the Future?

10. If we will choose to ignore the warnings of the _____ because we want to be like the nations around us in the _____ , no matter the cost, we will pay a _____ price.

View this teaching session at www.unshakenministries.com

Week Six: That My People Would Listen

This study is titled, "Journey Through the Psalms," and in the introduction we compared our time in the Psalms to a road trip. I have noticed patterns emerge when I travel with my family. The first stretch is exciting. It's ripe with possibility and excitement. It begins with a keen focus on the end.

Unfortunately, not long into the trip things can start to get tense. After being on the road for a while, the excitement wears off. Focus shifts from the destination to the vehicle itself. It can begin to feel like the mini-van is all that has ever existed and all that ever will exist.

Though we started with long-term vision, the duration of the trip has narrowed our gaze to the road directly in front of us and the condition of our immediate surroundings.

Suddenly, boredom, seemingly insignificant at the beginning, becomes an insurmountable obstacle stealing even the possibility of future joy. Our travelling companions have moved from tolerably quirky to unbearable. Rather than mere inconvenience, traffic jams and detours seem like reasons to abandon the trip altogether.

We are fickle travellers.

Our teaching session in Psalm 72 presented us with a refreshed vision of the final destination. A Righteous King will make the trip worthwhile and the journey bearable.

However, this week we will see that rebellion against our King will have far graver consequences than a couple of squirrely hours in a mini-van. Sin can drive the van into a ditch or spin it into a multi-car wreck.

This stretch of the journey will be tense. Yet let us not forget, when judgement and wrath meet us on the road, we can know that mercy and grace wait around the corner.

---

a WORD to the wise

LORD, I have heard of your fame;

I stand in awe of your deeds, O LORD.

Renew them in our day,

In our time make them known;

In wrath remember mercy.

Habakkuk 3:2 NIV

Day One: Is God My Comfort? (Psalm 73)

Road Trip Strategy #1: Comfort and distraction.

When we travel as a family, our goal is to keep the possibility of protest low by making sure the occupants are comfortable at all costs. If this is not possible, we distract the occupants from the knowledge that they are uncomfortable.

1. Read through Psalm 73.
    a. How are the wicked, the faithless, described in verse 4?

    b. How are the wicked dressed in verse 6?

    c. What is their condition in verse 7?

    d. What is the condition of their minds in verses 8-9?

    e. What response does this get from the people around them according to verse 10-11?

     f. What is appealing about the lifestyle of the wicked in verse 12?

    g. Is (or has) the lifestyle of the "wicked" been tempting or appealing to you? In what ways?

2. Turn to 2 Peter 2:12-14.
    a. How are the wicked described?

    b. According to verse 14, what kind of people do they entice?

 3. Read 2 Peter 2:18: How do the wicked entice in this verse and who are they enticing?

Can you see a common thread here? The faithless ones are distracted by their comfort. Most references to the wicked, or the faithless in the Psalms, refer to those who appear to belong to the covenant community but have not remained faithful to it. Covenant members who had been promised the best – the very presence of God – got so distracted by their desire for immediate comfort they forgot the reason they journeyed in the first place.

4. How is your desire for comfort compromising your focus on the destination?

There is the possibility that I could load my family in the mini-van and point it north for the ten-hour drive over the hills and through the woods to Nana and Papa's house, and make the trip so much fun nobody in the van remembers our purpose. I could placate every minor hunger pang with processed road-trip snacks so nobody has an appetite for the delicious home-cooked meal waiting for us when we arrive. I could stop for every road-side attraction along the way so that my family thinks they are having more fun on the trip itself than they will have at the destination. I could keep their video feeds streaming to the extent they've spent so much time with virtual personalities they aren't lonely for the real love waiting for them when we reach the end of the trip.

If the body of Christ will not get comfortable with being uncomfortable, or at least resigned to it, comfort will dictate conviction and result in a wreck of epic proportions.

 5. How might our fear of being uncomfortable hinder obedience to Christ?

6. What is God asking of you that you are hesitant to obey because it requires you to give up some form of comfort?

I am not advocating a mindset of being so 'heavenly minded we're no earthy good.' But seriously, how many people do you know where this is a possibility? Is not the greater danger of our times that we are so earthly minded we can't be used for any heavenly good?

7. Turn to Isaiah 53 and read through the chapter.
    a. How does the description of how the Messiah will appear in verse 2b compare with how the wicked clothe themselves in Psalm 73:6?

    b. How does the description of the Messiah in verse 4 compare with the description of the wicked from Psalm 73:5?

    c. How does the description of the Messiah in verse 5 compare with the description of the wicked from Psalm 73:4?

    d. How does the description of the Messiah in verse 7 compare with the description of the wicked from Psalm 73:8-11?

    e. What is the end of the matter for the Messiah and His followers in Isaiah 53:10-12 compared to the end of the matter for the wicked in Psalm 73:18-20, 27?

There is no better example of One who fixed His eyes on the destination, foregoing the comforts and distractions of immediacy, than our Saviour, Jesus Christ.

Talking to God:

Can we make the words of Paul in his letter to the Philippians our prayer today?

But whatever gain I had, I counted as loss for the sake of Christ. Indeed, I count everything as loss because of the surpassing worth of knowing Christ Jesus my Lord. For his sake I have suffered the loss of all things and count them as rubbish, in order that I may gain Christ and be found in him, not having a righteousness of my own that comes from the law, but that which comes through faith in Christ, the righteousness from God that depends on faith – that I may know him and the power of his resurrection, and may share his sufferings, becoming like him in his death, that by any means possible I may attain the resurrection from the dead.

Philippians 3:7-11 ESV

Day Two: Is God My Map? (Psalm 74)

Road Trip Strategy #2: Know where you are headed and have a plan for how to get there.

Early in our marriage, Rob and I spent a year living in England. A couple of months after arriving, we bought ourselves a very well-used Skoda for £100. It had been made in the country of Czechoslovakia (when it was still Czechoslovakia) and was constructed of solid steel. We affectionately named her Chitty Chitty Bang Bang, Chitty for short. Because her engine was under the back seat of the car, she rattled and bounced pleasantly as we drove. The previous owners informed us that while Chitty was reliable, she wasn't fast and shouldn't be driven more than 45-50 mph.

We spent many weekends putting lazily around the English countryside in our beloved Chitty. One Sunday afternoon we took her out for such a ride on country roads, no particular destination in mind. We drove aimlessly, chatting happily as she bounced. Our curiosity often led us down unfamiliar roads and this day was no exception.

Suddenly, our leisurely meander turned into a race not to get run over as traffic zipped around us. The road we had wandered onto had led to the Motorway. In desperation we coaxed Chitty to speeds she was unaccustomed to. The closer we got to 60 mph, the more smoke began to billow out from under the backseat. Chitty's endearing rattle began to sound like a death shudder and our cheerful comradery was replaced with frantic shouts of, "where are we," "how do we exit," and "will we survive until then?"

We wheezed and rattled down the first exit ramp we came upon, and spent the next part of the afternoon trying to find our way home. We could not go back the way we had come because of the danger posed by the Motorway, and we had no map to guide us down a new path.

We come to Psalm 74 and see the people of God lost and lacking direction. They have rebelled against the rule of their Righteous King and now face the devastating consequences.

 1. Read Psalm 74.
    a. What was the reason behind the dire situation the people of God were in?

     b. What were the consequences of this rebellion according to verses 3, 7, 8?

 2. Instead of the signposts of God's law, who was now providing direction according to verse 4?

    a. What was the condition of God's people according to verse 9?

    b. What was the condition of the land according to verse 20?

When the people of God stopped reading His signs and following His map, God stopped erecting the signs.

3. Are there signposts of God's law that you have stopped reading? What is keeping you from following them?

When we travel as a family, I have a habit that crops up as we come to the end of our journey. I tend to conclude our trip by giving my children a series of speeches. The nearness of the destination gets the kids all excited so I feel the need to channel their excitement productively with a review of expectation and protocol.

My speech follows a predictable pattern: *I know you're excited now, but when we arrive and they serve something for dinner that is unrecognizable and frightening to you, this is how you should respond. Or: when you encounter the temptation to run from the table to chase your friends, remember to stop and say thank you first.*

My reminders are often attached with warnings of consequences in the event that my children do not behave appropriately. Of course, the kids are quick to assure me that I'm crazy to think they won't be angels. I'm not easily convinced this will be the case and brace myself for inevitable breaches of protocol by my beloved offspring.

This is essentially what the book of Deuteronomy is: a series of speeches given by Moses to the people as they are about to enter the Promised Land. The people have wandered in the desert for 40 years, so to prepare them for their fresh start, Moses has a review session of protocol and expectation. Knowing they stand excitedly on the edge of the Promised Land, Moses takes the time to remind the people of how they had gotten it wrong in the past and urges them not to make the same mistakes again.

Deuteronomy is a map chock-full of relevant signposts.

4. Summarize in your own words the signpost given for the people to read and obey in each of the following passages:
    a. Deuteronomy 6:4-9

    b. Deuteronomy 8:2-3

    c. Deuteronomy 8:17-18

5. Read Deuteronomy 30:15-20: What reminder and what warning are given in this passage?

The people did not read the map and they ignored the signs. Their hearts rebelled against the Righteous King, so they became a nation that did not support righteousness and justice. Their leadership became a reflection of the people. Their rebellion kindled the anger of God against them and He allowed wicked nations to destroy them. Enemy powers occupied their land of promise. The temple of God's presence was profaned. God's right hand of power and favour stayed in His metaphorical pocket.

When people only listen to what they want to hear, there is the danger that only what they've listened to will speak.

6. Think of the people and influences in your life.
    a. Who or what would you say is the loudest voice? Explain.

 b. How does who or what you listen to influence the direction of your life?

7. Read Lamentations 2:8-9, 14: How did God punish His people in this passage?

The prophet Amos spoke a warning from the LORD about a coming day of bitter mourning.

"Behold, the days are coming," declares the Lord God, "when I will send a famine on the land – not a famine of bread, nor a thirst for water, but of hearing the words of the LORD. They shall wander from sea to sea, and from north to east; they shall run to and fro, to seek the word of the LORD, but they shall not find it."

Amos 8:11-12 ESV

The reign of the Righteous King in Psalm 72 was characterised by the King having dominion from sea to sea. The utter desolation of the day of bitter mourning is silence from sea to sea.

Talking to God:

Today's Psalm is an urgent warning to read the signs and follow the map on your journey. This week is the hard middle part of the road trip. The hours where we have lost some of the initial excitement of the journey, and cannot yet see the promise of arrival. But don't forget the promise we started with: where there is judgement and wrath, grace and mercy are around the corner.

Pray today that God would reveal His direction and His signs to you and that you would be obedient to His promptings. Pray also that His voice would be the loudest and most influential voice in your life. Thank Him that He is faithful to forgive and restore even the most broken amongst us.

Verse 12 of our Psalm today reads: *Yet God my King is from of old, working salvation in the midst of the earth.*

God is the Righteous King who delivers.

But God, being rich in mercy, because of the great love with which he loved us, even when we were dead in our trespasses, made us alive together with Christ – by grace you have been saved.

Ephesians 2:4-5 ESV

God always has a 'but' for the repentant heart that turns to Him.

Day Three: Has God Forgotten? (Psalm 77)

Road Trip Strategy #3: Know the purpose of your trip.

This past summer I took a trip. It was a purposeful trip. I needed to get away from the heavy stress of a particular situation and spend some time with family. I looked forward to the change of setting and being out of the reach of emails and phone calls. I was hoping for fresh eyes and clearer perspective.

But I forgot the purpose of my holiday. I forgot that I was intentionally getting away from emails and phone calls and decided to check them one last time before departing the world of internet connection. I forgot that my purpose was to achieve respite through distance and the distance became an irritant and an obstacle. I forgot that the distance was supposed to show me the situation was out of my control, and began to stress about how to control the situation despite the distance. Having lost sight of my purpose, I forgot that I had intentionally left things behind to enjoy a break and, instead of enjoying the break, I fretted about how to get things back.

We come to Psalm 77 today and repeatedly see the word, 'remember.'

Purposeful remembering is the antidote to forgetfulness.

1. Read through Psalm 77:1-9.
    a. What is the Psalmist remembering in verse 3 and how does it affect him?

     b. What is he remembering in verse 5?

     c. What is being actively remembered in verse 6?

The Psalmist is busy remembering, but he has a very big concern.

 2. In Psalm 77:9, what is the frightening possibility the psalmist considers?

The first part of Psalm 77 shows that the psalmist is crying audibly to God in the posture of persistent prayer. The psalmist is remembering God from a situation of deep trouble. As we have seen before in the Psalms, especially in Psalm 39, though the psalmists fear God, they do not fear bringing their big questions and strong protests to Him.

The LORD descended in the cloud and stood with him there, and proclaimed the name of the LORD. The LORD passed before him and proclaimed, "The LORD, the LORD, a God merciful and gracious, slow to anger, and abounding in steadfast love and faithfulness.

Exodus 34:5-6 ESV

3. By way of reminder, in Biblical time and culture, a name was a reflection of character. Read the verses from Exodus 34 above. These are the words of God as He proclaims His name to His people: what three phrases does He use to describe Himself?

4. According to Psalm 77:8, what does the psalmist fear has ended?

5. According to Psalm 77:9a, what does the psalmist worry God has forgotten?

6. According to Psalm 77:9b, what emotion does the psalmist worry will shut up compassion?

Do you see what the psalmist is questioning?!

The psalmist is remembering who God said He was, because he is worried God has forgotten.

All throughout the Psalms we have seen psalmists refer back to God's covenant and His promises as their assurance and security. In Psalm 77, we encounter the psalmist questioning this very foundation. What if God has forgotten? What if God has changed? If God won't keep His covenant, is the covenant pointless and God untrustworthy?

7. Read Exodus 15:6, 12: What does God's right hand represent and what does it accomplish?

8. Read Psalm 77:10: What is the psalmist appealing to?

The psalmist has the courage to remind God with an appeal. He appeals to God based on who God has said He is and how He has acted in the past.

> **O LORD, I have heard the report of you, and your work, O LORD, do I fear. In the midst of the years revive it; in the midst of the years make it known; in wrath remember mercy.**
> **Habakkuk 3:2 ESV**

9. Read Psalm 77:10-20.
   a. What two things is the psalmist remembering in verse 11 and 12?

   b. What statement are verses 13-15 making?

c. What point is the imagery of verses 16-18 making?

The psalmist remembers the deliverance of his people at the Red Sea and how it was a display of God's absolute power; nature responds to His authority.

 10. What conclusion does the psalmist come to in verses 19-20?

11. Have you experienced a time when God appeared unseen, yet looking back you can see His leading?

    a. What did God reveal of Himself to you in that experience?

    b. Would remembering who God is and all He has promised have changed anything for you during that time? Explain.

The psalmist has tossed in the dark of night, worried that God has changed, that God has forgotten. In response to this concern, he remembers the deeds of the Lord. Then he appears to end the psalm without a conclusion. There is no triumphant declaration of trust. There is only quiet acknowledgement.

Even when the footprints were unseen, God was with His people, leading them.

> **Can a woman forget her nursing child, that she should have no compassion on the son of her womb? Even these may forget, yet I will not forget you.**
> **Isaiah 49:15 ESV**

Perhaps in the psalmist's lack of conclusion, we see that the purpose has been in the act of remembering, itself. Perhaps in remembering his journey, the psalmist sees that the purpose of the journey is to reveal more of his ever-present companion. Perhaps, when it looks like He has forgotten, it is we who have.

Talking to God:

Lord God, in times of deep trouble we sometimes appeal to our own merit, our own worthiness, our own power. Turn our eyes from looking in or around, and instead may we look up. May we make our appeal to the years of your right hand. May we take the time to remember, to look back over our own lives. Give us eyes to see the times when you were walking beside us, times when you were leading, but your footprints were unseen. May our remembering give us confidence in your presence.

Day Four: Will God Restore? (Psalm 80)

Road Trip Strategy #4: Know the boundaries within which safety dwells.

With two of my siblings working in the field of mental health, I am hoping for a family discount when the time comes that my children need assistance getting over my imperfect parenting attempts.

Much of good parenting is about achieving balance. For example, when my children were young and strapped into their car seats, I tried to achieve the correct balance between making them aware of the seriousness of breaking travelling rules, without scaring them so much they were afraid to travel. As I tend to the dramatic, I got the balance wrong.

Wanting them to stay buckled, to keep their heads and hands away from open windows, and to ensure they never ever opened the door while the vehicle was in motion, I shared potential consequences of these actions. I thought nothing of seeing a hand out the window and shouting that people had lost bodily appendages that were dangling out the window, oblivious to the wide eyes in my backseat as I guided their imaginations to the possibility of an arm without a hand. I succeeded in making them aware of the potential danger, but when one of the four began to freak out every time someone reached towards the door, it seemed my warnings had tipped the scale too far in one direction.

God is a good Father; He has made clear the favour and safety we can experience if we journey with Him and the fearful consequences of travelling on our own.

1. Skim Deuteronomy 5:2, 6-22, and read Deuteronomy 29:1, 6, 24-29.
    a. What parameters did God place on His people?

    b. What were the consequences of living outside these parameters?

    c. What blessings were promised to the obedient?

God placed boundaries around His people because of His deep love for them and His desire to bless them.

The LORD spoke to Moses, saying, "Speak to Aaron and his sons, saying, 'Thus you shall bless the people of Israel: you shall say to them, "The LORD bless you and keep you; the LORD make his face to shine upon you and be gracious to you; the LORD lift up his countenance upon you and give you peace.'

So shall they put my name upon the people of Israel, and I will bless them."

Numbers 6:22-27 ESV

2. Read the blessing from Numbers above. These were the words the people of God heard before they left the tabernacle or the temple, the place where God's presence dwelled. In your own words, what five things did the Lord set upon His people as a blessing?

We come to Psalm 80, and find the people of God facing the wrath of God because they had abandoned the covenant they had made with Him. Instead, they had chosen to live outside the boundaries He had set.

3. Psalm 80 is a song that has a refrain (chorus) which is repeated three times. Read through Psalm 80 and take note of the refrain before answering the following questions.
   a. What is the psalmist asking of God before the first refrain?

   b. What is the psalmist saying between the second and the third refrain?

   c. Verses 14-15 are a variation on the refrain. Based on the refrain itself and this variation, what is the meaning of the refrain?

   d. What happened to the vine in verse 16a?

   e. What is the psalmist asking God do in response to that in verse 16b and 17?

   f. What does he say he and the people will do in verse 18 if God responds the way they've asked Him to?

God clearly placed safety parameters around His people's travels. We saw, just in the blessing from Numbers alone, that people who enter the presence of the Lord and look to Him for the blessing will receive it abundantly.

In Psalm 80:8-11, we read of an image that reoccurs in Scripture - the image of a vine. These verses show us that God carefully planted and cared for the vine, which symbolized the people of Israel, and He made it to prosper and grow.

4. What does the psalmist say that God has done in verse 12?

 5. Why did He do this? (Refer back to Psalm 80:4.)

The people of God did not want to dwell within the protective boundary God established for them, so He removed the protection.

6. Read Isaiah 5:1-7: In this Song of the Vineyard, the beloved is God and Israel is the vineyard.
    a. Summarize what the beloved did for the vineyard in verse 2.

    b. Write down the question raised in verse 4a.

    c. What will the beloved do according to verse 5-6?

As young toddlers, my children strained against the harness of their car seats. They found them too tight. Too constrictive. They wanted the freedom to move about as they pleased rather than being forcibly contained. I knew the value of the restrictions I placed around their travelling. It was for their own good.

God places boundaries around our travel time on earth. Protective walls to keep the enemy out so he cannot steal our fruit or ravage our vineyards. If we will rebel against this protection long enough, God will give us what we ask for. He will remove the protection He provides and leave us vulnerable, exposed to the enemy.

7. Are there parameters that God has set that you are rebelling against?

8. How might those parameters be a hedge of protection for you?

I am the true vine, and my Father is the vinedresser. Every branch in me that does not bear fruit he takes away, and every branch that does bear fruit he prunes, that it may bear more fruit. If anyone does not abide in me he is thrown away like a branch and withers; and the branches are gathered, thrown into the fire, and burned. If you abide in me, and my words abide in you, ask whatever you wish, and it will be done for you. By this my Father is glorified, that you bear much fruit and so prove to be my disciples. As the Father has loved me, so have I loved you. Abide in my love.

John 15:1-2, 6-9 ESV

Hear the judgement and the mercy in the words of the True Vine; apart from Him you do not travel in safety. Abiding in Him you will travel in safety, productivity, and love.

Talking to God:

Our Father is a good father; if the warnings are dire, it's because the consequences will be, too. Will you heed the warning of our loving Father and turn to Him? At the sound of your cry, He will turn to you.

Day Five: Oh, That My People Would Listen! (Psalm 81)

Road Trip Strategy #5: Having embarked on your journey, don't turn back.

I struggle with punctuality. I start with the best of intentions and prepare myself and my people ahead of time. But inevitably, moments before we actually have to leave, a distraction or an obstacle presents itself to delay our departure. And on those rare times I manage to get me and my people in the van on time, or even a touch early, we often don't drive very far before someone becomes aware of something they've forgotten and we have to turn back.

Leaving early and pointed in the right direction is of no benefit to us if what we've left behind pulls us back.

We come to Psalm 81 and immediately notice a significant difference compared to the other psalms we've looked at this week.

 1. Read Psalm 81.
   a. What is the difference?

   b. What might be the reason for this difference?

Most of the Psalms we have studied thus far have begun with a plea to listen or a cry for help. They come from a place of lament, or voice words of warning or judgement. Though they have had serious starts, many came to a 'but,' a place of hope before they ended.

Psalm 81 begins with a jubilant call to praise.

2. According to Psalm 81:4, why are the people of God to sing aloud and shout for joy?

This is not a random encouragement to praise based on feelings or circumstances. It is because God has told them to. I'm curious, did you react to that sentence?

3. Is your praise and worship of God primarily based on feelings and circumstances? Explain.

4. Does it change things for you to know that praise and worship of God is required by God?

If we look at Psalm 81:3, we see that the psalmist has a very specific reason and occasion for his instruction to worship.

5. According to verse 3, at what two times were they to blow the trumpet?

In establishing covenant with His people, God instructed them to observe specific feasts at specific times and in specific ways. God set aside the seventh month of the year as holy. On the first day of the seventh month, the day of the New Moon, the people were to celebrate the Feast of the Trumpets. They were not to do ordinary work, but to blow the trumpets and present burnt offerings. (Numbers 29:1-6) On the fifteenth day of the seventh month, the day of the full moon, God's people were to celebrate the Feast of Booths.

6. What significant day fell in between these two feasts according to Leviticus 16:29-30?

The first ten days of the seventh month were the holiest days of the year. They began with the Feast of Trumpets, which marked the end of one harvest season and the beginning of another, and ended with a day where the Israelites came before God to present offerings and sacrifices for sin. These ten days were set aside for people to search their hearts and confess their sin.[12]

 7. The holiest days of the year began with the blowing of trumpets. What was the purpose behind this sound? (Numbers 10:9-10)

The sound of the trumpet was a reminder to God to remember His people. Psalm 81 begins with a triumphant call to praise in verses 1-3 because, as we see in verses 4-7, God did remember His people. Psalm 81 is reminding the people that, at a time when they called out to God in distress, He delivered them. He answered them even though they tested Him.

8. What promises do you need to be reminded of today?

9. In what ways has God been faithful to you in fulfilling His promises?

---

[12] ESV Study Bible, page 312

10. What location is referred to in Psalm 81:7?

 11. Read Exodus 17:7: With what question did the people of Israel test God?

After opening with a call to praise and a reminder of great deliverance, Psalm 81 then moves to a declaration from God.

12. How does God admonish His people in Psalm 81:8?

13. What does God declare in Psalm 81:10?

 14. What is the turning point of verse 11?

In most of the other Psalms we have looked at, the 'but' signals a turn from despair to hope, from doubt to faith, from disobedience to repentance. In this Psalm, it does not. This Psalm starts from a place of joy and recounting powerful miracles; despite this, there is a 'but.' There is a turning. God reprimands His people: "If only you'd listen to me! If you would follow my commandments, worship me, look only to me for your good, I would fill you to overflowing!"

BUT

God's people didn't listen or submit.

SO

God gave them over to their own way.

IF ONLY

If only they would listen, God would give them the very best and satisfy them.

But this command I gave them: 'Obey my voice, and I will be your God, and you shall be my people. And walk in all the way that I command you, that it may be well with you.' But they did not obey or incline their ear, but walked in their own counsels and the stubbornness of their evil hearts, and went backward and not forward.

Jeremiah 7:23-24 ESV

God's people started out with praise and celebration, remembering how faithful He had been to them. But as the excitement of the journey waned, they turned back to their old ways and forgot the covenant they had made with their God. We, too, can begin our journey with the best of intentions but get sidetracked, distracted, and turned around. As we are pulled and swayed by the influences of this world, we stop listening to God's voice and instead follow the desires of our flesh. May it not be said of us that we started well, but did not finish.

Talking to God:

A somber Psalm such as this one can begin joyfully because there is joy in knowing that even the hard words from God are a mercy. They are the bright caution signs along the way that make us aware of important and needful route recalculations. Even His judgement is grace. Bring your journey to God today in self-examination. Are you walking in all the ways that He has commanded, or are you trying to supplement His directions with some of your own? Allow Him to adjust your route where needed. In His infinite love and mercy, He will keep you driving forward and guide you to your destination.

DIGGING DEEPER: Covenant God

Intro & Definition of Covenant

If you've grown up in the church or are familiar with your Bible, you've probably heard about covenants. You may even be familiar with some of the particular covenants God established with His people, or with well-known phrases like 'God of the Covenant,' 'God is faithful to His covenant promises,' 'God established a New Covenant with His people,' or 'Jesus is the fulfillment of the Old Covenant promise.' The problem with familiar terms is that we think we understand the meaning, make assumptions and sometimes miss the point entirely. So what is God's message in the covenants? And what is the magnitude of His covenant promises?

The Merriam-Webster Dictionary defines covenant as:
1. a usually formal, solemn, and binding agreement
2. a written agreement or promise usually under seal between two or more parties, especially for the performance of some action

The problem with this definition, when we talk about covenant between God and man, is the term "agreement." Agreement usually assumes some sort of negotiation which leads to agreed-upon or accepted terms between two parties. This is not the case with God. God comes to us on His terms not ours. He comes knowing what we need, what is best. He comes with the covenant already established. We choose whether or not to enter in. We choose to accept the terms or not.

Description of the Covenants:

It is important that we understand the different covenants God made with His people throughout Scripture. The message of the covenants is woven throughout the entire Bible and therefore to properly know and understand the message of Scripture we must know and understand the promises of the covenants.

In our study of the Psalms, we've seen references to many major Old Testament themes as well as reminders of the promises made in the Abrahamic, Mosaic, and Davidic covenants. We read of God's faithfulness, His trustworthiness, and His goodness. We read how He is true to His promises. A closer examination will deepen our understanding.

Abrahamic Covenant:

Go from your country, your people and your father's household to the land I will show you. I will make you into a great nation and I will bless you; I will make your name great, and you will be a blessing. I will bless those who bless you, and whoever curses you I will curse; and all peoples will be blessed through you…Look up at the sky and count the stars – if indeed you can count them…So shall your offspring be…I am the LORD, who brought you out of Ur of the Chaldeans to give you this land to take possession of it…To your descendants I give this land, from Wadi of Egypt to the great river, the Euphrates.
Genesis 12:1-3; 15:5,7,18 NIV

God not only initiated covenant with Abraham, He attached three promises to the covenant: the promise of land, the promise of a great nation, and the promise of blessing and redemption (Gen 12:1-3).

God would fulfill each of these promises in His timing. He would use human hands but divine intervention would be needed. And Abraham, in faith, would need to trust God and wait.

In Genesis 17, God comes to Abraham again and reaffirms the covenant. God promises that a nation will be built up through the descendants of Abraham. As a physical sign of the covenant, God required that Abraham and every male among him who was eight days and older be circumcised. Circumcision was not a foreign practice to people of that time or culture, however it was usually performed during adolescence. God required it of infants to show that all fruitfulness, all life, came through Him.

In Genesis 21, Abraham and his wife Sarah welcome their son, Isaac. The fulfillment of God's promise. They respond in obedience, circumcising Isaac on the eighth day as God commanded. But Isaac is just one son. God promised descendants as numerous as the stars in the sky. Abraham did not waver in his faith. He understood the concept of patience. Fulfillment would not happen in his lifetime. God's plan was an eternal one and Abraham played a small but important role. Abraham now stands for all generations as a witness, a hero of faith. He shows us how to live by faith. For Abraham's faith was not in himself or even in the promise, but in the One who had made the promise and would faithfully see it to completion.

With man this is impossible, but with God all things are possible.
Matthew 19:26 NIV

Mosaic Covenant:

You yourselves have seen what I did to Egypt, and how I carried you on eagles' wings and brought you to myself. Now if you obey me fully and keep my covenant, then out of all the nations you will be my treasured possession. Although the whole earth is mine, you will be for me a kingdom of priests and a holy nation.
Exodus 19:4-6 NIV

After rescuing His people from slavery in Egypt and leading them safely through the Red Sea, God made a covenant with Moses and the people of Israel on Mount Sinai. This covenant was to set Israel apart from the other nations as God's chosen people and to prepare them so that God's presence could dwell among them.

God promised His blessing, but it was conditional on obedience. God promised His presence, but parameters were set. For Holy God to dwell among sinful humanity, conditions must be met. But in His mercy, God showed His people the way to enjoy His presence among them. He gave the people a set of laws to follow in the form of the Ten Commandments. He showed them how to live and govern themselves in a right and just manner. He set out laws of justice, mercy, and social responsibility. He created laws for the protection of people and property. He clearly set out the requirements for sacrifice and worship. He gave detailed instructions on how the Tabernacle, His dwelling place among them, should be built leaving nothing out. Dimension. Material. Placement. God also laid out the consequences for disobedience.

When Moses went and told the people all the LORD'S words and laws, they responded with one voice, 'Everything the LORD has said we will do.'
Exodus 24:3 NIV

But the weight of the covenant proved too heavy for the people. For generations to come, the Israelites would need to be reminded that the animal sacrifices were not performed out of duty or tradition. The shedding of animal blood was meant as a daily reminder of their sin. It was meant to signify contrite hearts. Hearts that understood on a daily basis their need for God's saving grace. God didn't want their sacrifices. He wanted their hearts. Hearts that sought to obey Him fully. Hearts that served Him faithfully. The blood was a reminder of this. But the blood of animals did not offer salvation. That required a Perfect Sacrifice.

'The time is coming,' declares the LORD, 'when I will make a new covenant with the people of Israel and with the people of Judah. It will not be like the covenant I made with their forefathers when I took them by the hand to lead them out of Egypt, because they broke my covenant, though I was a husband to them,' declares the LORD. 'This is the covenant I will make with the people of Israel after that time,' declares the LORD. 'I will put my law in their minds and write it on their hearts. I will be their God, and they will be my people. No longer will a man teach his neighbor, or a man his brother, saying, 'Know the LORD,' because they will all know me, from the least of them to the greatest,' declares the LORD. 'For I will forgive their wickedness and will remember their sins no more.'
Jeremiah 31:31-34 NIV

Davidic Covenant:
This is what the LORD Almighty says: I took you from the pasture and from following the flock to be ruler over my people Israel. I have been with you wherever you have gone, and I have cut off all your enemies from before you. Now I will make your name great, like the names of the greatest men on earth. And I will provide a place for my people Israel and will plant them so that they can have a home of their own and no longer be disturbed...I will also give you rest from all your enemies. The LORD declares to you that the LORD himself will establish a house for you: When your days are over and you rest with your ancestors, I will raise up your offspring to succeed you, your own flesh and blood, and I will establish his kingdom. He is the one who will build a house for my Name, and I will establish the throne of his kingdom forever. I will be his father, and he will be my son...Your house and your kingdom will endure forever before me, your throne will be established forever.
2 Samuel 7:8-16 NIV

God entered into covenant with David and reaffirmed the promise made to Abraham. The promise of a home for His people. God further promised that within the security of a nation, there would be security of succession. A king from the line of David would remain on the throne forever. Within this promise of secure and permanent dwelling, God established that His dwelling would move from the transient Tabernacle to a permanent Temple. David's son Solomon would later build the Temple according to God`s instruction. And again, though human hands were used, God was doing the building. God would build a royal house for His Name. God would build His kingdom. And this kingdom would be established forever.

The promise of permanent dwelling and unending rule foreshadowed another Son who would come from the line of David.

For to us a child is born, to us a son is given, and the government will be upon his shoulders. And he will be called Wonderful Counselor, Mighty God, Everlasting Father, Prince of Peace.
Isaiah 9:6 NIV

Jesus: The New Covenant

And you are heirs of the prophets and of the covenant God made with your fathers. He said to Abraham, 'Through your offspring all peoples on earth will be blessed.' When God raised up his servant, he sent him first to you to bless you by turning each of you from your wicked ways.
Acts 3:25-26 NIV

Abraham never wavered in believing God's promise. In fact, his faith grew stronger, and in this he brought glory to God. He was fully convinced that God is able to do whatever he promises. And because of Abraham's faith, God counted him as righteous. And when God counted him as righteous, it wasn't just for Abraham's benefit. It was recorded for our benefit, too, assuring us that God will also count us as righteous if we believe in him, the one who raised Jesus our Lord from the dead. He was handed over to die because of our sins, and he was raised to life to make us right with God.
Romans 4:20-25 NLT.

In the Abrahamic Covenant, God promised to bless all people through the seed of Abraham. This promised seed was Christ Jesus, God's Son. Through Him we are blessed. Through Him we have forgiveness of sin. Through Him we have life.

This child who was born centuries after Abraham lived, would one day hang on the cross with the weight of our sin on His shoulders. His death and resurrection would remove the barriers that once existed between us and the Father and unite us with Him for all eternity. Through Christ, we would become sons and daughters of the One True King. United in one body and one Spirit, with one God and father who is over all and in all (Ephesians 4:4-5). We who have faith are descendants of Abraham. As numerous as the stars in the sky.

For Abraham is the father of all who believe.
Romans 4:16 NIV

In the Mosaic Covenant we see God open the eyes of His people to their need of a Saviour. He made a way for them to atone for their sins through the sacrifice of animals, the shedding of blood. And He promised to dwell among them.

But God knew His people. He knew their fickle ways. He knew they would forsake Him and break covenant with Him.

And the LORD said to Moses: 'You are going to rest with your ancestors, and these people will soon prostitute themselves to the foreign gods of the land they are entering. They will forsake me and break the covenant I made with them. And in that day I will become angry with them and forsake them; I will hide my face from them, and they will be destroyed.'
Deuteronomy 31:16-17 NIV

The people were unable to obey the law on their own. The blood of animals was not able to save them, only appease God's wrath. God planned a better way from the beginning. A perfect way. A mediator to stand between the people and God.

We have this hope as an anchor for the soul, firm and secure. It enters the inner sanctuary behind the curtain, where our forerunner, Jesus, has entered on our behalf. He has become a high priest forever, in the order of Melchizedek…Now the first covenant had regulations for worship and also an earthly sanctuary…the priests entered regularly into the outer room to carry on their ministry. But only the high priest entered the inner room, and that only once a year, and never without blood, which he offered for himself and for the sins the people had committed in ignorance…But when Christ came as high priest of the good things that are now already here, he went through the greater and more perfect tabernacle that is not made with human hands…He did not enter by means of the blood of goats and calves, but he entered the Most Holy Place once for all by his own blood, thus obtaining eternal redemption…For this reason Christ is the mediator of a new covenant, that those who are called may receive the promised eternal inheritance – now that he has died as a ransom to set them free from the sins committed under the first covenant…For Christ did not enter a sanctuary made with human hands that was only a copy of the true one; he entered heaven itself, now to appear for us in God's presence. Nor did he enter heaven to offer himself again and again, the way the high priest enters the Most Holy Place every year with blood that is not his own…so Christ was sacrificed once to take away the sins of many; and he will appear a second time, not to bear sin, but to bring salvation to those who are waiting for him.
Hebrews 6:19-20, 9:1,6-7,11-12,15,24-25,28 NIV

Jesus is our High Priest. He is our Perfect Sacrifice. His blood was poured out so we might have life. He stands as the mediator between us and God, offering us relationship with the Father. He is the fulfillment of the promised blessing to Moses. And He is the promised blessing to us today.

Jesus is also the fulfillment of the Davidic Covenant. God promised David that his kingdom would endure forever before Him, and his throne would be established forever. When the angel Gabriel appeared to Mary to announce the good news of great joy, these were his words…

Do not be afraid, Mary; you have found favor with God. You will conceive and give birth to a son, and you are to call him Jesus. He will be great and will be called the Son of the Most High. The Lord God will give him the throne of his father David, and he will reign over Jacob's descendants forever; his kingdom will never end.
Luke 1:31-33 NIV

For no matter how many promises God has made, they are 'Yes' in Christ. And so through him the 'Amen' is spoken by us to the glory of God.
2 Corinthians 1:20 NIV

Conclusion

Hebrews 11, often referred to as The Faith Chapter, gives powerful examples of Old Testament saints who never saw God's fulfillment of His promises.

These were all commended for their faith, yet none of them received what had been promised. God had planned something better for us so that only together with us would they be made perfect.
Hebrews 11: 39-40 NIV

These are some of the promises we've been given in Christ: Relationship with the Father. Unconditional love. Forgiveness of sin. Freedom from condemnation. Eternal hope. Eternal life. God is faithful. He will keep His covenant. In Abraham, Moses, David, and so many others throughout Scripture, we have powerful examples of faith from those who never saw the fulfillment of the promise but still believed!

Therefore, since we are surrounded by such a great cloud of witnesses, let us throw off everything that hinders and the sin that so easily entangles, and let us run with perseverance the race marked out for us. Let us fix our eyes on Jesus, the author and perfecter of our faith.
Hebrews 12:1-2 NIV

From Abraham through to the promised Son, God has proven His faithfulness. With such a history of fulfilled promises, we can trust that He will do what He says. We may not see the fulfillment in our life time. We may not understand the working of His hand. But we can know and trust the One on whom the promise rests.

Know therefore that the LORD your God is God; he is the faithful God, keeping his covenant of love to a thousand generations of those who love him and keep his commandments.
Deuteronomy 7:9 NIV

Psalm 89: Listening Guide

Turbulence:

- Biblical Literacy: Though available in abundance, are we consuming life-giving spiritual food?

- Empty Words: Because we do not eat real, solid, filling words, we are seduced by empty words that tickle our ears.

- Famine in the land: Amos 8:11-12.

Signs of the Time:

- Are we uncomfortable with being uncomfortable? Do we want to play?!

- Deprived of information or drowned in information?
    Truth concealed or drowned in irrelevance?

- Captive culture or trivial culture?
    No freedom to choose alternatives, or concerned only with trivial or unimportant things.

- Post-modernism: The shift from 'God' to 'I'
    Distrust of meta-narrative (the big story).

View this teaching session at www.unshakenministries.com

Answers for the Time:

- God of the Covenant
  Who has God said He is?

- Songs in the light and songs in the night
  The only way the people of Israel knew how to make sense of pain and suffering.

- Stepping stones
  The faithful are content to be stepping stones because they know they are part of a bigger story.

- Psalm 89
  o What I know to be true (verse 11)
  o What has He done (verse 10)
  o Who our God is (verse 14)
  o What does this mean for His people (verse 15)

- A remnant

For I know whom I have believed in, and am persuaded that He is able. To keep that, which I've committed, unto Him until That Day!

2 Timothy 1:12 ESV

View this teaching session at www.unshakenministries.com

Week Seven: The Lord is King!

This week of study marks our arrival at the turning point of the Psalms. We have journeyed through songs, prayers, and poems that, despite coming from places of trouble and distress, projected confidence and trust in the God of the covenant, no matter the circumstances.

But Book Three took a sharp turn, past the point of confidence and into a place of hard questions and pervasive doubt. God's people raised serious questions. They had been promised a king from the line of David who would be on the throne forever, and that there would be a king who reigned in righteousness and justice. This was not their reality. Most of their kings did not rule well; they chased after desire rather than righteousness and justice was sold to the highest bidder.

As Book Three draws to a close, it appears the covenant has been abandoned by both parties. Israel was a nation divided. Both the Northern and the Southern kingdoms looked more like the nations around them than like a people set apart to showcase the glory of God. Their kings were conquered, their people scattered, and deep darkness and disillusionment threatened the people of God. Exiled from home, there was no one to lead them.

The people of God needed direction. Someone to guide them. Someone to remind them.

We come to Book Four which opens with a psalm of Moses. Book Four points readers back to a time when Israel did not have a human king but to a time when God was their King. It is a reminder that God was working on behalf of the faithful long before King David.

Yahweh reigns! is the consistent refrain. It is the truth that contests the darkness and disillusionment of the people. If the faithful were tempted to look for their security in a human king, even one from the Davidic line, they would be disappointed.

Only one point of confidence is enduring hope for the faithful: God the great King.

---

a WORD to the wise

The kingdom of the world has

become

the kingdom of our Lord and of his Christ,

and he will reign for ever and

ever.

Revelation 11:15b NIV

Day One: Do You Know the Time? (Psalm 90)

Rob and I have been married for twenty years and sometimes I feel like it has been a two-decade-long game of 'What's the Time, Mr. Wolfe?' If you're not familiar with the game, the basic premise is that Mr. Wolfe always knows what time it is. The other players attempt to determine the time, because in this game, time dictates behaviour.

Rob lives with a strong need for punctuality. I see the value in punctuality but struggle to achieve it. As you can image, this is a source of tension in our marriage. Rob frequently asks me if I know what time it is, not because he doubts my ability to tell time, but because he doubts my ability to respond appropriately.

Too many times I have been found reading a book ten minutes before we need to leave, despite an earlier warning about the time. Too often I have dismissed his reminders with a casual, "Thanks, Hon, I'm ready to go," before going right back to my book. This results in a marked increase in Rob's stress level because he knows from past experience that in the final moments before departure, I will feel caught off guard by the immediacy of the time. I will worry about arriving at my destination unprepared so am likely to run to the bathroom for last minute touch ups and adjustments. Thus, despite best intentions, we will be late.

I say I am ready, but I am complacent. I say I know what the time is, but my actions do not reflect this.

Awareness of time should impact behaviour.

After the disorienting darkness of Book Three, Book Four of the Psalms opens with a Psalm about time. Psalm 90 is a time-check: know the time, respond accordingly.

1. Begin by reading through all of Psalm 90, and then come back to the first two verses:
    a. What does the first line of verse 1 tell us that God is to His people?

    b. According to the second line of verse 1, how long has this been the case?

    c. How long has God been God, according to verse 2?

2. What is the condition of mankind, according to Psalm 90:3-6?

3. According to Psalm 90:7-10, what is the reason for our condition?

4. How does Genesis 3:17-19 further expand your understanding of this?

5. Read Psalm 90:11 slowly and several times.
   a. What is it saying?

   b. Flip to Exodus 20:20. The word 'fear' is used paradoxically in this verse. How does it contribute to your understanding of Psalm 90:11?

6. Psalm 90 is attributed to Moses, the man of God. In Psalm 90:12, Moses arrives at the lesson of the Psalm. It is a response to his knowledge of who God is, his knowledge of what man is, and his knowledge of the reason for our condition. Write the lesson of Psalm 90:12 in your own words.

7. How does a right understanding of verse 12 impact our actions and our response to God?

Moses begins his Psalm with what he knows to be true about God. (By the way, that is always the best starting point!) For a man who spent a great portion of his life without a home, Moses has experienced the truth of God as his home - a safe place to dwell. He was a first-hand witness to the power of God over creation through the mighty plagues in Egypt and the deliverance at the Red Sea. Moses saw the provision of God with bread from heaven and fresh water from rocks every day of his 40 years of wandering. Moses had walked with his God and knew who He was.

Moses then moves to what he knows to be true about himself. Though called a man of God, he had murdered someone in an act of rage. Though called to lead God's chosen people, he protested against this calling and would only step out in faith when God provided him with a human assistant. Though a mediator of God's grace to His people, Moses' anger over their stubborn rebellion caused him to cry out, "Hear now, you rebels: shall we bring water for you out of this rock?" (Numbers 20:10) and then to hit the rock twice after God specifically told him to speak to it. Moses knew his sinful condition.

After leading difficult people through decades of testing and tribulation, and seemingly pointless wandering in a desert, I can only imagine that Moses, standing at the edge of the Promised Land, tasted a measure of futility. For him, the journey's destination would only be seen from a distance and never entered. It must have felt like his life was ending with only a sigh when it could have been with a shout.

Who understands the power of Your anger? Who connects this brevity of life among us with Your judgment of sin? And your wrath, who connects it with the reverent fear that is due You?

Psalm 90:11 AMP

Verse 11 is the truth that brings Moses to the lesson of verse 12. In our sinful condition, we fail to see the reason for our mortality and so we are tempted into living selfishly for the moment or succumbing to pointlessness and despair. We fail to see the importance of time, and how it should impact our behaviour.

Moses, however, learned the lesson of numbering his days through a right knowledge of who God is, who mankind is, and the truth of the human condition.

8. What does Moses look to for satisfaction in Psalm 90:14?

9. Whose work is Moses wanting on display in verse 16?

10. Why do you think Moses prays this?

11. How does Moses conclude the Psalm in verse 17?

Moses sees that God is not standing outside of time, He is standing in all of time.

The eternity of God is not merely the opposite of the brevity of mankind, it is the answer to it.[13]

 12. What connection do you see between the conclusion of Psalm 90 in verse 17, and the encouragement of Paul in 1 Corinthians 15:58?

When we face the difficult facts of time, judgement, and death, we are met with a wonderful paradox. By acknowledging that our lives are fleeting, we can be cured from the disease of

---

[13] Kidner, Derek. <u>Kidner Classic Commentaries</u>, Psalm 73-150, © Inter-Varsity Press, London, 1975, pg 359.

living only for the moment. Dwelling in God, though we are transient and brief, we can work with purpose and favour on that which will last for eternity.

But do not forget this one thing, dear friends: With the Lord a day is like a thousand years, and a thousand years are like a day. The Lord is not slow in keeping his promise, as some understand slowness. Instead he is patient with you, not wanting anyone to perish, but everyone to come to repentance.

But the day of the Lord will come like a thief. The heavens will disappear with a roar; the elements will be destroyed by fire, and the earth and everything done in it will be laid bare. Since everything will be destroyed in this way, what kind of people ought you to be? You ought to live holy and godly lives.

2 Peter 3:8-11 NIV

Talking to God:

In the passage above, Peter calls believers to action. He reminds them that awareness of time should impact behaviour. As you come to eternal God, our dwelling place, answer the question of Peter. How is your awareness of time affecting your behaviour? Are you asking for the favour of God to be upon the work of your hands, and are you looking to Him to establish your work?

Day Two: The LORD Reigns! (Psalm 93)

Almost every September I am filled with a renewed desire to organize my life. I am inspired by the pretty agendas and day-timers on sale, sucked in by images of 30 days of slow-cooker eating, 30 days of school lunches, 30 days to a clean home on my social media feed . . . I'm convinced I must impose this order upon my life and all that I see inspires me to believe it is possible.

My laptop spits out colour-coordinated chore charts for everyone in the family. I gather my people around me and feed their meal ideas into a spreadsheet - 30 days of meals as well as weekly grocery lists.

Summer chaos falling into the order of autumn delights me and I follow my lovely charts for a while. When I obey the dictates of the day I can be confident that laundry will be done on Monday, groceries will be bought on Tuesday, floors vacuumed on Wednesday . . . My family is confident they will be fortified in their work with healthy and wholesome meals. The announcement of cereal for supper will be a cry unheard in our home.

The thing is, as wonderful as my charts can be (I have created beauties!), they are only of value when I follow them. When they get forgotten in the busyness of life, we return to questions, like, "Will there be clean socks for everyone today or does the cleanest child have to recycle his?" Or, "Will there be fresh fruit for everyone's lunch or will someone have to hold scurvy at bay with a dried fruit bar?"

Order brings stability to our lives.

The chaos of Book Three is answered by the order of Book Four. It is a coming back to what the faithful knew to be true, a way of living they knew to be secure. It opens with the re-orientation of Psalm 90; God's eternity is the answer to our mortality. Psalm 91 follows, a tender psalm of confidence in the loving protection of God, who is a safe dwelling place. And then we have Psalm 92 and 93. These songs were supposed to be sung on specific days of the week; there was order to their placement. Psalm 92 is a boisterous hymn of praise and thanks that was to be sung on the Sabbath, and Psalm 93 is a declaration of Kingship to be sung the day before the Sabbath.

 1. As you prepare to read Psalm 93, consider that this short psalm, rich in imagery, was meant to be sung on the sixth day of the week. What do you think the purpose of this was?

a. Verse 1 is a breathtaking image of a King and how He is dressed. What two items of apparel does the psalmist describe and what do those images convey to you about the King?

b. After describing Yahweh, the psalmist ends verse 1 by describing the world. What does he say about it?

c. The psalmist is still describing in verse 2. What does he describe and how is it described?

d. Note: there is important repetition from verse 1b and 2a. What word is repeated? What does it describe in 1b and what is it describing in 2a? What do you think is the significance of this?

Okay, before finishing the psalm, let's pause for a bit. The picture of Yahweh as King that the psalmist paints is a pretty specific one, so we want to make sure we are seeing it clearly.

2. Turn to Isaiah 51:9: What is the author asking God to do in this verse? (Just as an aside, the reference to Rahab and the dragon in this verse are both symbolic references to Egypt.)

Isaiah asks God to dress Himself for battle on behalf of His people; Yahweh responds by promising that His salvation is coming.

3. Read Isaiah 52:7.
    a. What is the good news that is being announced?

    b. Which descriptive words in this verse give us a picture of the good news?

The picture in Isaiah is one of a runner sprinting towards a city that is in despair over what they thought was inevitable defeat. Instead they hear the runner shouting jubilantly, "Your God reigns! Your King was victorious!"

The opening three words of Psalm 93 are conveying that same picture. They are not merely a statement, they are an announcement. Yahweh reigns! He reigns in majesty, and in power as a strong warrior.

The throne of the King is established, therefore the world is established and shall never be moved.

Psalm 93 was sung on the sixth day. We read in Genesis 1:24-31 that this was the day God filled up the earth with living things. In many previous psalms, we have seen the psalmists deriving security from looking back at God's work on behalf of His chosen people.

This psalm is looking even further back than that. This psalm is saying that Yahweh, Covenant God, was King over creation long before His chosen people were even on the scene. When "the earth was without form and void and darkness was over the face of the deep," (Genesis 1:2) God was there. He was the King who ruled even then, bringing order from chaos.

4. How does this reminder instill confidence in us?

5. Continue reading Psalm 93, picking up at verse 3.
    a. What mighty force is lifting up its pounding in verse 3?

    b. What is the declaration in verse 4?

6. Turn to Genesis 1:9-10.
    a. What is God's command in these verses?

    b. Read Job 38:8-11: What is God describing to Job?

    c.   Flip back to Genesis 9:11: What covenant does God make with Noah?

To the people of Israel, there was no more vivid symbol of chaos than a raging sea. There was no more insurmountable force than the force of nature. The psalmist declares that even when the waters threaten to overwhelm the land, God puts them in their place. As mighty and powerful as the sea is, Yahweh is more so.

    7.   Read the conclusion of Psalm 93 in verse 5. What is the psalmist describing and how does he describe each one?

    8.   What do you think the Psalmist is saying here?

    9.   What attributes of God's character do you see described in this Psalm?

The true glory of God is not just in His majesty or His power, it is in His character.

God created and filled the earth and He ensures it is a safe place to dwell. He is King over the chaos of nature. He is majestic in power and might. He is a God of order. The order He imposed on the universe reveals He is trustworthy and reliable. The order He gave in His law revealed His character; He is as beautiful and trustworthy as His law.

And now I am about to go the way of all the earth, and you know in your hearts and souls, all of you, that not one word has failed of all the good things that the LORD your God promised concerning you. All have come to pass for you; not one of them has failed.

Joshua 23:14 ESV

Psalm 93 begins to beat a steady refrain that is continued through most of Book Four. The LORD reigns. The King is on the throne. Yahweh reigned as King over creation and He will be King forevermore. We can experience stability because of the order imposed by our King.

Talking to God:

God has the power to establish the created world securely because His throne is established securely. If our universe is held secure by our King, you can be assured that your world is secure in His hands too. We can say with Paul, "all the promises of God find their Yes in Jesus. That is why it is through him that we utter our Amen to God for his glory." (2 Corinthians 1:20-21) Jesus Christ is the ultimate promise of the Scriptures. His throne is firmly established in power and victory. Our God reigns!

Day Three: Come Let Us Worship (Psalm 95)

Where I come from, hockey is a big deal. Most people have basic knowledge of the game, but for many it goes way further than that. They are true fans of the game. Born and raised in Alberta, hockey fans have two choices: the Edmonton Oilers or the Calgary Flames. The rivalry between the two teams is intense.

I am a Flames fan. There hasn't been a lot to cheer about through the years. My team tends to the mediocre. Not bad enough to get first round draft picks (ahem, Oilers fans I'm calling you out) but after the Stanley Cup win of 1989, not good enough to get past the first round of the playoffs.

Until 2004. That was the year my team qualified for the playoffs for the first time since 1996. That was the year they defeated three division winners on their way to the Stanley Cup Finals. That was the year unlikely heroes emerged and unsung heroes finally earned the recognition they deserved.

It was the year my rather apathetic support became ardent. I went from knowing a handful of players at best, to knowing entire lines. That was the year I watched their games with my own eyes, rather than being content to hear about them second-hand. It was the year I turned from a fan to a follower. When they lost in a heart-breaking game seven of the final series, I cried.

For about ten minutes. And then I went back to my regular life. I forgot the names of the players. I stopped watching their games. Reports of wins or losses didn't provoke much emotion in me.

I am related to many Oilers fans, through birth and through marriage. My brother is the most zealous of them all. Two years after my team's run for glory, his team squeaked into the Stanley Cup playoffs. As underdogs, they surprised fans with dogged determination and steady advancement. All the way to the Stanley Cup Finals.

When my team was in the finals, I was excited. I watched the games. I even paid a bit of money to go watch them on the big screen at our local football stadium. But I didn't get a jersey. I didn't inconvenience my schedule. I was only in it for the fun.

When my brother's team was in the finals, he sacrificed for his team. Though a poor college student, he scraped his money together to go to watch them play in their stadium. He already had the jersey. They were his schedule. He loved it for the fun, but was in it for life.

When his team lost in game seven of the Stanley Cup Final, it cut deep. He cried for a while, but then he picked up the pieces and went back to his regular life. More armchair coaching. Continued speculation on possible draft picks and line reconfigurations to give them a better chance next year. He cheered them through their victories, but didn't forget them after their losses. No matter how difficult the season, he clings to the hope that this might be the year.

True worship is devoted.

What does this battle of Alberta hockey story have to do with our study in the Psalms? Let's see.

1. Read Psalm 95.

    a. What is the reader invited to do in verse 1?

    b. What is the reader invited to do in verse 2?

Did you notice the repetition? Twice the psalmist encourages the reader to enter the presence of God with noise. The verb used is one that comes from everyday language and not from religious language. It's a verb that means noise – not necessarily joy filled or anger filled, just loud.[14]

That's my brother at an Oilers game. Loud. Celebratory when appropriate and upset when needed, but just plain loud because it matters to him. He is the fan shouting loudly during the games no matter what is going on.

I am the fan sitting in my seat with a wandering eye. I people watch; I plan my snack schedule; I mentally re-design the stadium for greater comfort. Sure, I cheer when they score, but sometimes I have to watch the goal on the big screen because I missed it on the ice. I wasn't paying attention to the game itself; I was distracted by the side shows.

My brother's heart of devotion is displayed in his actions. My apathetic heart is displayed in mine.

True worship has a fervour that can't be faked.

2. According to verses 3-5, what are the reasons for our loud entrance into the presence of God?

3. Based on what you've read in verses 1-5, what do you imagine is the posture of the worshiper?

4. Now turn to verse 6. The encouragement to come and worship gets more specific.

    a. What is the posture the psalmist encourages the worshipper to take before God?

    b. What reason do you see for adopting that posture in verse 5?

---

[14] Baker Commentary page 90

The opening verses of Psalm 95 are the call to come and worship. We are to come as true 'fans.' Not preoccupied or complacent, but engaged and ardent. We are coming into the presence of our Creator King! We can come boisterously and confidently, but when we come with engaged awareness it will lead to a posture of lowering ourselves before Him.

5. How aware are you in the presence of God?

6. How does an increased awareness lead to changed behaviour and actions?

7. Fill in the blanks for verse seven (taken from the ESV): For he is _____ God, and _____ are the people of _____ pasture, and the sheep of _____ hand.

8. What do you notice about the words you filled in?

Do you know why my brother is so invested in his team? Because he really sees it as *his* team. He interacts on the fan websites. He follows tweets and twitters, but more than that, he engages in it with comments of his own. Both their defeats and their victories are his. It is personal to him because he feels an acute sense of belonging.

God the great King is the God over creation, but He is also the personal God of His people.

A more literal interpretation of verse seven is "Because he is our God and we are the people he pastures, the sheep in his hand."[15] We are the people He pastures. We are the sheep in His hand.

Psalm 95 has been setting its readers up for the turning point, which is the last line of verse seven.

9. Write down the last line of verse 7, underlining the first, third, and fourth words (from the ESV).

Psalm 95 says if you're going to be a true worshipper, come before the presence of your Maker like you mean it. Listen. Respond.

10. What is the response encouraged by the psalmist in verse 8?

---

[15] Ibid, pg 93

Massah means testing. It was the place in the wilderness where the people of God complained they were thirsty. They did not express confidence in God's provision but rather tested Him by asking if He was with them or not. (Exodus 17:1-7)

11. What does the psalmist say the people did in verse 9?

The people of God did not take Him at His word or believe the proof of His works.

They paid the price for their doubt and unbelief.

12. In what ways do your actions and attitudes express confidence in God's provision?

13. In verse 10, God calls out His people for two things. What are they?

14. What was the result according to verse 11?

Verse 11 refers to an oath God made in response to His people's reaction to the spies' report of the Promised Land. When they heard 10 of the 12 spies convey fear over the size of the occupants, they cried and wept and grumbled. "Why couldn't we die in the wilderness instead of dying by the sword? they wondered." (Numbers 14:1-3)

15. What is God's response to their complaints in Numbers 14:28-30?

16. Look back at the last line of verse 7 and the first part of verse 8. _____ if _____ hear his voice, do not harden _____ hearts.

17. After looking at the passage in Numbers, does it change your understanding of the tone of this warning? Explain.

The warning was not just for the people of Israel; it is for us too. If there is any doubt in your mind about it, see this. A portion of Psalm 95 is quoted five times in the span of two chapters in the book of Hebrews, with the line above quoted three of the five times. (Hebrews 3 & 4) The author of Hebrews warns his readers of the consequences of unbelief, but also points them to faithful acts of obedience and the resulting blessings.

Christ is faithful over God's house as a son. And we are his house if indeed we hold fast our confidence and our boasting in our hope.

Hebrews 3:6 ESV

18. According to the verse above, we are his house if what?

True worshippers are not like fair-weather fans. They stay the course and maintain their confidence.

19. Flip to Hebrews chapter 3 and note verse 6 and 7. The author of Hebrews follows this by restating the warning for the people of his day. Read Hebrews 3:12-13: What is the warning?

Therefore, while the promise of entering his rest still stands, let us fear lest any of you should seem to have failed to reach it. For good news came to us just as to them, but the message they heard did not benefit them, because it did not meet with faith in the hearers . . . Let us therefore strive to enter that rest, so that no one may fall by the same sort of disobedience

Hebrews 4:1-2, 11 ESV

Psalm 95 is challenging its readers to enter the presence of God in true worship. You might say you are one of God's people, but will you behave like one? You might say you're a fan, but does it impact your actions when the celebration is over? It should. Because for true fans, the celebration hasn't even started yet. There remains the promise of a Sabbath rest in the pasture of His hand for eternity!

Talking to God:

Father, knowing that we have a standing invitation to enter Your presence, may we do so with the same noisy anticipation of true fans entering a stadium. May we focus on the reason we come rather than the side shows which only distract our attention from You. Because it's personal, may we hear and respond to Your voice in true faith and heart driven worship. Give us perseverance and endurance in knowing that You started the work and You will finish it, once and for all in Your presence when we join you in the Sabbath rest that completed the work of creation and will complete the work of redemption.

Amen

Day Four: Worship All the Earth (Psalm 96)

Psalm 93 established that God is King because He is Creator; all that we see is under His rule of authority because He is the author of it. (Did you notice that?! The word authority has 'author' as the root word!)

Psalm 95 calls the people of God to praise Him because He is their King. He is the God of the covenant and the covenant people.

That seems kind of limiting to those of us who would not be considered one of the original covenant people. And when you consider that the people of Israel were a small nation compared to the rest of the peoples of earth, and Yahweh is just King over His people, then He is a small King of a small people. Perish the thought! Psalm 93 has already pointed us to the fact that Yahweh is creator of all, therefore He is King of all. If there is any doubt left in your mind, read Psalm 96.

1. In Psalm 96:1-2, the psalmist asks the reader to sing three times.
   a. Sing what? (verse 1a)

   b. Who should sing? (verse 1b)

   c. What is the content of the song? (verse 2)

2. What is to be declared in verse 3?

   a. Who is it to be declared to?

   b. Why? (verse 4-6)

If we could understand Hebrew, which is the language the Psalms were written in, we would notice a fun little play on words in verse five. In Hebrew, the words 'gods' (elohim) and worthless idols (elilim) sound alike. If we were to translate the first phrase from verse five into English, we would say something like, "These mighty beings, are mighty useless."[16] Yahweh is the only Creator, so while people may have the misguided perception that there are other gods, even if they existed, they would be worthless and powerless in the face of the One who made all.

All that exists is His and He should get all the credit.

---

[16] ESV Study Bible page 1060

That's what the next stanza is all about. The word 'ascribe' means to give credit where it belongs. The credit should be given to Yahweh, the God of Israel, who is the God of all creation.

3. Who is instructed to give the credit to Yahweh in verse 7?

4. What is the invitation extended in the second part of verse 8?

Did you get that?! I wonder what Jewish people thought when they read Psalm 96:8. You see, there was an inscription on the wall of the outer courtyard of the Jerusalem temple warning Gentiles that they would only have themselves to blame for their death if they passed beyond it into the inner courts.[17] And yet the Israelites sang the words of Psalm 96. Words like *all the earth, among the nations, all the peoples*. Words that invite all the earth to bring an offering and enter His courts! Do you think they wondered what that was all about?

5. What common thread do you see in the following verses?
    a. Genesis 12:3

    b. Psalm 22:27-28

    c. Isaiah 2:1-2

    d. Isaiah 11:9b-10

    e. Habakkuk 2:14

The opening word in the second stanza of Psalm 96:2 is a word that means 'take the news.' It is the verb which gives us the word 'evangelize.'[18] The good news that Yahweh reigns was never meant to be kept quiet. This good news was always intended to be spread into all the world.

6. Turn to Romans 10:11-13. Who is the good news for?

7. Continue reading in Romans 10:14-15. What is the issue raised in these verses?

---

[17] ESV Study Bible page 2265
[18] Kidner Classic Commentaries, Psalm 96 page 379

Did you notice Paul quoted Isaiah 52:7 here (from our homework on Day 2)? *How beautiful upon the mountains are the feet of him who brings good news, who publishes peace, who brings good news of happiness, who publishes salvation, who says to Zion, "Your God reigns."* The good news is described as news of peace, happiness, and salvation because God reigns!

God's plan was always that His chosen people would evangelize – would spread the good news of His saving work.

8. Re-read the conclusion of Psalm 96 in verses 10-13.
    a. What is the message in verse 10?

    b. Who is declaring the message and how? (verses 11-12)

    c. Why are they rejoicing? (verse 13)

    d. What do verses 11-13 tell us about how we should declare the coming of Christ? How should we testify?

Isn't that exciting?! God's people are not to view evangelism as a dour task, or a duty to be fulfilled. Spreading the good news that God reigns is to be the natural overflow of true worshippers. We are to be like the true fan that can't keep our enthusiasm quiet; we have to let it out. We are to be people that have a new song on our lips. Not necessarily songs that are new in content but songs that are new in experience because we have had fresh encounters with the Living God!

9. What fresh encounter with the Living God is spilling out to those around you?

10. How can you encourage these fresh encounters in your life? What steps are you taking to keep a new song on your lips?

What is the cause of the great joy of the people of God?

He comes.

Blessed is the King who comes in the name of the Lord! Peace in heaven and glory in the highest!

Luke 19:38 ESV

The day that Jesus rode into Jerusalem on a donkey, multitudes rejoiced and praised God with a loud voice. Their King had come and they could not be silent. When the Pharisees asked Jesus to silence His disciples, Jesus answered,

I tell you, if these were silent, the very stones would cry out."

Luke 19:40 ESV

The LORD reigns! The King comes!

Remember that inscription in the temple that separated the Jews from the Gentiles? Matthew 27:51 says that the moment Jesus died, the curtain in the temple was torn in two from top to bottom. The King had come and torn down what divided people from Him. This is the good news that is for all people.

But now in Christ Jesus you who once were far off have been brought near by the blood of Christ. For he himself is our peace, who has made us both one and has broken down in his flesh the dividing wall of hostility.

Ephesians 2:13-14 ESV

Talking to God:

As you come to God today, thank Him for the reconciliation He brought about with the sacrifice of His Son. Thank Him that because of Jesus, all people can experience the Good News of Salvation and be welcome in His presence.

Now live like there is no barrier between you and God. Live like you have the joy of Salvation and spread it to those around you.

Day Five: The LORD Reigns (Psalm 97)

We should not be surprised at how our Psalm today opens.

1. Read Psalm 97:1.
   a. What does the opening phrase establish as a fact?

   b. As a result of this, what two things respond and how?

Isn't this a wonderful summary of our week as a whole? Because the LORD reigns as King, creation itself rejoices and peoples from distant shores are glad.

2. Before we go any further into our Psalm today, pause for a moment and examine your heart. How does the knowledge that God is your King encourage you? Strengthen you?

Embolden you? Does it make your heart glad and cause you to rejoice? Why or why not?

The question above is the type of question where it seems like there is a 'right answer' that you should write down. Don't worry about that. God doesn't need to read what you've written on paper; He sees your heart. If the answer of your heart is not the 'right answer,' take it to God. As we've moved through the Psalms, we've seen that He wants honesty more than empty piousness.

3. Continue reading through Psalm 97.
    a. What is the tone of the message in verses 2-6? What images are conveyed?

    b. What is the tone of the message in verses 8-12? What images are conveyed in this passage?

    c. What is the message of the connecting verse? (verse 7)

    d. What event in Israel's history does the imagery in verses 2-3 bring to mind?

You might have read these verses and recalled that when Yahweh led His people out of slavery in Egypt, He went before them in a pillar of cloud by day and a pillar of fire by night. (Exodus 13:22) Throughout history God frequently appeared in this manner. Why is this?

The cloud and the fire of God's presence served two purposes.

4. Read Exodus 40:32-38.
    a. After Moses had finished the work, what filled the tabernacle?

    b. How were the people of Israel protected by the cloud? (Hint: what was the cloud covering?)

    c. Summarize the conclusion to the book of Exodus by putting verse 38 in your own words.

And the LORD said to Moses, "Tell Aaron your brother not to come at any time into the Holy Place inside the veil, before the mercy seat that is on the ark, so that he may not die. For I will appear in the cloud over the mercy seat.

Leviticus 16:2 ESV

The first purpose of the cloud was that it protected the people from the intensity of God's holy glory. Do you remember when Moses asked God to show him His glory in Exodus 33:18? God answered Moses by saying, "You cannot see my face and live." (Exodus 33:20) In His sweet mercy and tender love, God gives us a glimpse of His holiness to draw us to Him and to ignite within us a reverent fear of Him. Yet, at the same time, He shields us from the fullness of His glory so we may live.

The second purpose of the cloud was that it preserved some of the mystery of God. 1 Corinthians 13:12 says that now we only see dimly and we only know in part. When we see Him face to face we will see clearly, and we will know fully as we are fully known.

For now, we live with mystery. But one day, God's glory will be revealed.

A voice cries:

"In the wilderness prepare the way of the LORD; make straight in the desert a highway for our God. Every valley shall be lifted up, and every mountain and hill be made low; the uneven ground shall become level, and the rough places a plain. And the glory of the LORD shall be revealed, and all flesh shall see it together, for the mouth of the LORD has spoken."

Isaiah 40:3-5 ESV

John the Baptist quoted these verses when the people asked him who he was. Was he Elijah? Was he the Messiah? John says, "No. I'm the voice crying out in the wilderness as a warning; God's glory is going to be revealed."

5.   What is said about Jesus in John 1:14?

Jesus came in the flesh to pitch His tent among us. That's what the phrase 'dwelt among us' means. Just as the glory of God dwelt among His people in the tent that served as their tabernacle in the wilderness, Jesus put on the tent of human flesh to dwell among us. But the glory of Jesus wasn't recognized by many. Why? He was fully God, but He was fully man. Humanity was the cloud that obscured the fullness of His glory.

For a time.

6.   Hours before going to the cross, what did Jesus pray for His followers in John 17:24?

Jesus knew His glory would only be fully revealed at the conclusion of the redemption story. But He couldn't wait for that time. He couldn't wait for the day his followers would finally see clearly. He couldn't wait for the day that they would see him, whom they only knew obscured by the cloud of flesh, revealed in the fullness of His glory as the Son of God. Let's look ahead to the conclusion of the redemption story in Revelation.

7. Read Revelation 19:11-16.

    a. What is the name of the one seated on the horse?

    b. What is on His head?

    c. What will He do? (verse 15)

    d. How will He rule? (verse 11)

    e. What name is written on His robe and on His thigh?

The LORD reigns! He is the King above all kings and the Lord above all lords. There is no power on earth that can rival this King. For those who submit to His reign, there is joy because He is a faithful and trustworthy King. For those who think they reign, the imminence of the coming King is a worrying fact.

This is where the two-fold purpose of the fire of God comes in.

8. Read 1 Corinthians 3:11-15: What two things will God's fire accomplish?

9. What is the result of this testing? (verses 14 & 15)

God's fire will either consume or refine and reveal. Because this is true, how do we respond? This brings us to the exhortation of Psalm 97.

10. What does the psalmist urge readers to do in Psalm 97:10a?

    a. What does God do for those who are obedient? (verses 10b & 11)

    b. How are we to respond to God's faithfulness? (verse 12)

Then the seventh angel blew his trumpet, and there were loud voices in heaven, saying, "The kingdom of the world has become the kingdom of our Lord and of his Christ, and he shall reign forever and ever." And the twenty-four elders who sit on their thrones before God fell on their faces and worshiped God, saying,

"We give thanks to you, Lord God Almighty, who is and who was, for you have taken your great power and begun to reign. The nations raged, but your wrath came, and the time for the dead to be judged, and for rewarding your servants, the prophets and saints, and those who fear your name, both small and great, and for destroying the destroyers of the earth."

Then God's temple in heaven was opened, and the ark of his covenant was seen within his temple. There were flashes of lightening, rumbling, peals of thunders, an earthquake, and heavy hail.

Revelation 11:15-19 ESV

Talking to God:

We began today with examining our hearts and how they respond to the knowledge of God as King. This might feel scary, but remember, God our King rules in righteousness and justice, and Jesus came to impart His perfect righteousness to us, and to pay the price that justice demands. Knowing this, ask God to send His Holy Fire to refine and purify you. Ask Him to prepare you for the fullness of His presence and to fill you with joy over the anticipation of being with Him where He is and seeing His glory.

CALL TO PRAYER

It is difficult for us humans to comprehend life outside of the confines of time. We are bound by its realities. The sensation of never having enough hours in a day to get the jobs done, yet desiring for time in the waiting and longing seasons to speed up, while yearning for time's deteriorating effects to decelerate before wreaking havoc in us. Culture encourages us to "live in the moment" or to "be present," while hypocritically demanding that we do more, spend more, 'be' more. It's exhausting and damaging. I wonder at the "idol" we have made of our own busyness. An idol can be something that I 'worship' or something that I've become a slave to; something that no longer serves me, but rather, I serve it. In essence, it becomes my master. It takes God's rightful place in my heart and mind. I have been humbled and repentant in the way I sometimes talk about my schedule - like it controls me as opposed to the other way around. Father, forgive me.

Like me, I imagine you have experienced seasons of waiting - periods of unknowns, times of liminality. Liminal spaces are those in-between moments - moments where we stand on the threshold of something new, something unknown. A place between the familiar and the uncertain. A time of discomfort, waiting, and transformation. Liminal spaces are places where God is at work, yet we often fail to see it. Like me, you may have longed to hurry through to the other side. Maybe you have spent much too long crying out to God, "How long O Lord?!" desperate for the waiting to be over. And yet, these are the places God grows us- the places God reveals Himself to us - the places we can see and know His faithfulness. But... we must choose to see - choose our perspective.

Like me, maybe you have noticed the trampling of time across your features (when did I start having to hold up my eyelids in order to put on mascara without it smudging?) Like me, maybe you have come to realize that seasons of waiting are inevitable. It's in these times that I am desperate for the truth that God is not limited by time nor adversely affected by its passage. "Jesus Christ is [eternally changeless, always] the same yesterday and today and forever." Hebrews 13:8 AMP. He is sovereign over time universally, sovereign over the waiting, and even sovereign over my daily schedule.

Practice

In this week's homework, we considered God's eternal presence and provision in Psalm 90. We approached the question of how an awareness of time should affect our behaviour. Living our lives in Christ permits us the gift of eternal perspective. Eternal living begins at the moment we begin life anew in Christ Jesus.

Ecclesiastes 3:11 says [God] has put eternity into man's heart. We were meant to live with this perspective in mind. Awareness regarding the brevity of life on earth should urge us to live out God's will with a sense of purpose. This eternal perspective should impact what we prioritize and it should impact our actions based on the fact that we are not powerless when in Christ – we have His victory.

But first, we must see. We must recognize and be aware of all we've been given in Christ. Ephesians tells us we have access to every spiritual blessing in Christ: His power, His spiritual riches, and inheritance - we don't HAVE to wait! These things are for us even now! He equips us to live heavenly kingdom lives in Christ even while we are yet bound by earthly realities. When we fail to see our inheritance in Christ, when we fail to utilize it here on earth, we tend to lose sight of the Father's workings in our lives and, instead, prioritize that which is fleeting. May we instead pray daily that our eyes would be opened to the spiritual blessings we've been given. May we apply them in our daily living and in doing so, claim the victory He has already won. Matthew 6:21 tells us that our heart is where our treasure is. When our treasure is with God - when we are living in light of eternity - the things of this world and the ways of this world lose their appeal and we begin to prioritize that which is lasting (eternal).

Like the Israelites, however, we have a tendency to forget; forget who we are in Christ and all that we have in him. Amidst the urgency of our to-dos, we forget eternity. That is why Paul reminds us in Ephesians to be made new in the attitudes of our minds (4:23). We must renew our minds in Christ Jesus daily, hourly, and some days even minute by minute. The opposite of forgetting is remembering, but not just passively. We need to activate our minds, purposefully place our attentions on heavenly things, and remove our attention from earthly things (Colossians 3:1,2). Like Abraham, we can learn to refocus our eyes from the discouraging moments in front of us to look upward to the heavens and declare the majesty and promises of God. God's covenant to Abraham, where He promised to give him descendants as numerous as the stars and bless them through him, seemed like an impossibility unless he was looking up. The lens of eternal perspective is based on the knowledge and truth of the God revealed to us in the Scriptures.

We are not called to live for the moment but to seek God in each moment. In this way we can rejoice in both the good ones and the damaged ones (Philippians 4:4). As Psalm 90:12 asks God to teach us to number our days that we may cultivate wisdom, we, too, can do this by seeking Him and then thanking Him and praising Him. In our moments, He reveals Himself and we respond to His presence within us. "'For in him we live and move and have our being.'..." Acts 17:28. As we abide in Christ and as surely as His Spirit abides in us, we can live purpose-filled lives, joy-filled, grace-filled Godly lives. He gives us our moments to prepare us for His presence. As we submit our hearts and minds to Him, He sanctifies us.

On Our Knees

"...Be still, and know that I am God; I will be exalted among the nations, I will be exalted in the earth.'" Psalm 46:10. The word 'be still' comes from the Hebrew word 'raphah' and suggests a dropping of hands or 'chilling out'. Contextually, the verse implies that God is able, despite our inabilities or insurmountable circumstances. Our response can be calm and confident because we continually tune in to God's intervention on behalf of mankind throughout the ages. We develop this eternal perspective through continual, purposeful reflection. We can be still because we KNOW who God is.

Thank God for who He is and for His Word that reveals this knowledge. Thank Him for this knowledge revealed through the life of Jesus, and for the knowledge and insight revealed by the indwelling of His Spirit in our hearts.

Ask God to teach you to number your days with gracious and grateful hearts. Ask Him to reveal Himself to you in the moments of your day. Ask Him to be your vision that you may gain eternal perspectives in the midst of the temporal. Ask Him to give you knowledge and depth of insight as you seek Him in all things, developing a Biblical fear of Him and cultivating wisdom. Ask Him to fill you so full of gratitude and grace that His gospel message cannot be contained within you, but overflows to those around you. Thank Him for His timeless gospel and that His redemptive plan involves the passing away of sin and brokenness and heartache and pain, and that eternity will be marked by His perfect presence. "So we fix our eyes not on what is seen, but on what is unseen, since what is seen is temporary, but what is unseen is eternal." 2 Corinthians 4:18

How does God want you to respond to this knowledge of Him? How is He calling you to submit your time and your schedule to Him? How does He want you to use the time He is entrusting to you?

Turn your eyes upon Jesus
Look full in his wonderful face
And the things of earth will grow strangely dim
In the light of his glory and grace

Turn Your Eyes Upon Jesus - Helen H. Lemmel 1922

Psalm 98: Listening Guide

Reason for the Song:

1. We are invited to sing because our King has _____!

Content of the Song:

2. God has worked _____.

3. God has _____ His salvation.

4. His salvation is for _____ and has been _____ to everyone.

5. If God will _____ His salvation to all people, He will _____ it to all people.

View this teaching session at www.unshakenministries.com

Implications of the Song:

6. If the song of salvation is for_____, then _____ should join in the song.

7. When God does His_____, we should _____.

8. We do not get to _____ and _____ who we think is _____ to hear the song of salvation.

Week Eight: If God is King . . .

Our homework last week started in Psalm 90 where we saw that we act on what we believe to be true. The rest of last week was spent looking at God as King.

Encountering the truths of God should transform us, not just inform us. If we truly believe God is King above all kings, there is an implication for us. This is where our focus turns this week.

If God is King . . .

---

a WORD to the wise

The fear of the LORD is the

beginning of wisdom;

all who follow His precepts

have good understanding.

To Him belongs eternal praise.

Psalm 111:10 NIV

Day One: Integrity in My House (Psalm 101)

After reading the short introduction to this week of study, we want to get right into Psalm 101. We want to let it hit us between the eyes. Because it's likely to.

Let's begin with a quick orientation in regards to context: Psalm 101 is what is called a royal psalm. Royal psalms set the leadership standard. Royal psalms speak to the manner in which the kings of Israel were to rule over God's people. Keeping this in mind, we will read Psalm 101 to see the standard it sets forth.

1. Read through Psalm 101 and fill in the chart below:

I will . . . (verse1)	
I will . . . (verse 2)	
I will . . . (verse 2b)	

I will . . . (verse 3)	
I will . . . (verse 4b)	
I will . . . (verse 5a)	
I will . . . (verse 5b)	
I will . . . (verse 6)	
I will . . . (verse 8)	

Did you complete the chart and feel like Psalm 101 left much wiggle room? Nope. Neither did I. Psalm 101 can not be called ambiguous. Let's dig a little deeper into this psalm of David who, if we remember, is the standard other kings of Israel were held to.

2. What is David pondering in verse 2a? (ESV)

    a. How is David committing to walk in 2b?

    b. In verse 6b, David is committed to receiving counsel from what kind of person?

The words or phrases you just isolated are all interpreted from the same word meaning, integrity.

in•teg•ri•ty

the quality of being honest and having strong moral principles, moral uprightness; the state of being whole and undivided; internal consistency or lack of corruption

from integer

in • te • ger

a whole number; a number that is not a fraction; a thing complete in itself

 3. As you read the definition for the word 'integrity' and its root word 'integer,' how do you see their meanings expand the theme of Psalm 101 and relate to the standard of kings of Israel?

Looking into our futures, I imagine very few of us see the possibility of royalty. Many of us will not lead large corporations, never mind entire nations. But we all have the capacity and opportunity for leadership. In our homes. In our friendship groups. In our areas of service. The leadership profile of Psalm 101 is for more than just the kings of Israel.

4. Using Psalm 101 as a guide, conduct a performance review of your leadership. In what areas do you think you are doing well? Which standards from Psalm 101 do you need to improve on?

Being presented with the standard, and examining your own performance can be discouraging, can't it? You're not alone.

Psalm 101 sets forth a standard of ideals. The true story of the author's life casts the shadow of reality over these ideals.

The Bible doesn't hide the reality of the human condition under ideals. One of the great examples of the Bible giving us both the standard and the reality is in the life of King David. The book of 2 Samuel tells much of his story, and there we see that though his heart chased after God's, his reality was still marred by sin.

5. If you are familiar with the life of David, jot down what you know about his story. In what ways do you see that he lived by the standard of Psalm 101? (If you are not familiar with David's life, skim read the following references for some help: 2 Samuel 11, 2 Samuel 13:1-22, 2 Samuel 14:28-15:6)

a. In what ways did he not live by the standard of Psalm 101? What were the consequences?

b. How and where do you see lack of integrity leading to fracturing and brokenness rather than wholeness in David's life? In his home?

A life of integrity protects against fracture and division.

Integrity starts on the inside and works its way out. Wholeness grows within the walls of our hearts, and then our homes, and then it spills out of us onto the people in our lives. Fractured living does the same.

God is King; He reigns in righteousness and justice and absolute integrity. That leaves serious implications for us and how we choose to live our lives.

The second phrase of verse two seems like a random question. Almost like it interrupts the flow of the psalm itself.

 6. What do you think is the meaning or purpose of that phrase? What do you think it is pointing you to?

In Psalm 101, David makes a poetic declaration of commitment to the standard of righteousness required of the kings of Israel. But he cries out to God, *"Oh when will you come to me?"* because David knew he was incapable of fulfilling the requirement set. He knew there was only one way in which he could live up to the expectations placed on him - through the sustaining help of God.

When we hold ourselves up to the light of the perfect standard of righteousness on our own merits, we see our deeply shadowed and darkened reality; we need God. We need saving. Jesus met the standard of perfection that we could not.

Within the context of it being a royal psalm, we see that Psalm 101 is the standard of a righteous king. *Within the context of Book Four of the psalms, we see that only God, the Righteous King, can meet this standard.*

Talking to God:

Only Jesus Christ, the Righteous King, meets the perfect standard of righteousness. While teaching His disciples, Jesus said,

Unless your righteousness exceeds that of the scribes and Pharisees, you will never enter the kingdom of heaven . . . you therefore, must be perfect, as your heavenly Father is perfect.

Matthew 5:20, 48 ESV

But the only perfection we can attain is the righteous perfection of Christ given to us by Him. That is our only hope. Oh but it is a sure hope!

Compose a psalm of your own today. A psalm that follows in the pattern of Psalm 101, and sets forth the standard by which you will govern your life. A psalm that affirms that 'God is the Righteous King so this is how I will live my life.' And then ask Him to help you do it.

Day Two: Give Thanks for His Steadfast Love (Psalm 106)

Today we will be studying Psalm 106, the psalm that concludes Book Four. It is the last of a series of historical psalms; psalms that recount events from the past as a reason to celebrate who God is, what He has done, and anticipate what He will do. Psalm 106 has also been called a hymn of praise, but once you start reading it, you might wonder why. If you've already turned to Psalm 106, you've noticed that it is a psalm of some length. We don't want to get lost in it so will read and respond to it in sections.

1. Read Psalm 106:1-5: What are two reasons for giving thanks to the LORD in verse 1?

2. Verses 4-5 are a personal interlude. What does the psalmist ask of God in these verses?

   a. In God's community, the individual is not lost in the crowd. Is knowing that you are not lost in the crowd a comfort to you, or more of a discomfort? Would you rather be lost in the crowd or known despite a crowd? Why? Glance ahead. How does God respond to this prayer in verses 44-46?

   b. What does this response reveal about our God?

Read verse 6 out loud, and more than once because this verse is the point that must be kept in mind as the rest of the psalm is read.

Before beginning to list the sins of the fathers, the psalmist wants readers to be crystal clear: 'we' are not separate from 'they.' Their story is ours.

3. Read verses 7-13.
    a. What two things did the people of Israel forget to do according to verse 7?

    b. Is this a problem of the mind or the heart?

    c. According to the last phrase of verse 7, what action did this lead to?

    d. What did God do for the Israelites in verse 8 despite their rebellion, and why?

    e. What was the Israelites' response in verse 12?

    f. What did the Israelites do in verse 13?

Do you see a pattern emerging here? As we look at the history of the Israelites, we see them crying out to God to be rescued. We see God respond in power and might, displaying His works for all to see; rescuing His people. We see the people of God rejoicing and singing His praises. And then we see them forget God and go their own way.

This was the pattern of the Israelites, but it is also the pattern of us. Remember what verse 6 makes clear? This is not just a 'they' problem. It is our problem too. It is the problem of our hearts. That is why Proverbs 4:23 instructs us to guard our hearts above all else. Everything we do flows from it. What we believe in our hearts is what we trust to be true. Therefore, it influences our actions. The Israelites failed to trust God when they couldn't see His plan. They let their fear dictate their response. They chose to see with their eyes instead of believing with their hearts.

Chronic unbelief leads to acts of rebellion . . .

4. Read verses 13-18.
    a. What two things did 'they' do according to verse 13?

    b. What does verse 14 say the people did?

    c. What do you think was at the heart of their testing?

d. What heart problem did the people of Israel encounter according to verse 16a?

On the night that Jesus was handed over to Pilate by a much later generation of Israelites, Pilate tried to convince them not to crucify Jesus because he knew Jesus was innocent. *For he [Pilate] knew that it was out of envy that they [the Jews] had delivered him [Jesus] up. Matthew 27:18* The inclination of our hearts has not changed in the two thousand years since that night. The same selfish tendencies and sinful desires that nailed Jesus to the cross are evident in us today. That is why we must continually cry as David did, *Search me, O God, and know my heart; test me and know my anxious thoughts. See if there is any offensive way in me, and lead me in the way everlasting. Psalm 139:23-24*

Where jealousy takes root, a spirit of discontent grows.

5. Read verses 19-23.
   a. What did 'they' do next according to verses 19-20?

   b. Why did they do it? (verse 21)

   c. In the ESV, verse 23 begins with the word 'therefore.' What is it there for? How will the situation of verses 19-22 lead to the situation in verse 23a?

   d. Verse 23 tells us that God wanted to destroy the Israelites because of their actions. The second line in verse 23 begins with the words, 'had not.' What happened to prevent this?

We see a similar situation in the book of Ezekiel. God is looking for someone to stand in the gap and intercede. *And I sought for a man among them who should build up the wall and stand in the breach before me for the land, that I should not destroy it, but I found none. Therefore, I have poured out my indignation upon them. I have consumed them with the fire of my wrath. I have returned their way upon their heads, declares the Lord GOD. Ezekiel 22:30-31* In this instance, there was no one found to stand in the gap and intercede.

God is looking for godly men and women to stand in the breach and intercede, but when we, like the Israelites, allow other things to take God's rightful place in our lives, we become unable to satisfy this calling. May it not be said of us that there was no one found!

6. Read verses 24-27: These verses refer to the days when the people whom God had delivered from Egypt and led through the wilderness stood on the edge of the land He had promised to them. They heard reports from ten spies: there are giants in the land and they are too big for us to defeat.
    a. What was at the heart of the people's fear according to verse 24?

    b. How did their actions display their beliefs according to verse 25?

Lack of faith in the promises of God can lead to complaining and disobedience.

7. Read verses 28-31.
    a. What did the Israelites do in verse 28?

    b. What was the response of God, the great King, in verse 29?

    c. How was God's wrath averted according to verse 30a? (Two things)

We will become tied to whatever we are tempted to worship in the place of God and so we will not be free to stand in the gap and intercede.

8. Read verses 32-33.
    a. What did they do according to these two verses?

When our behaviour provokes those in authority over us to anger, or steals their joy, the body of Christ is not built up as He desires it to be.

9. Read verses 34-39.
    a. What did the Israelites not do according to verse 34?

    b. What did they do instead, according to verse 35 & 36?

When we mix the purity of God's commands with the ways of the world, we exchange the greatness of what God has given us for something lesser.

10. Read the conclusion of Psalm 106 in verses 40-48.

Psalm 106 opened with praise and thanks for the character of the great King - steadfast, unending love. The remainder of Psalm 106 recounts how, though the people had such a King, they didn't want to submit to His authority. They wanted to do it their way. God gave them what they wanted. Verse 41 says God handed them over to the nations they were trying so hard to live with and to be like. God gave them what they wanted and they willingly exchanged the rule of the King of love for the rule of nations who hated them. They exchanged a King of righteousness and justice for the rule of those who oppressed them and who cared nothing about right or just living.

This was 'their' cycle; they rebelled and then faced the consequences. When the consequences were painful and difficult, they cried for God to save them. And He would. And then they began their cycle again. And many times He delivered them.

How is Psalm 106 a hymn of praise? Because the wonder of this psalm, a psalm that recounts the consistent and deliberate cycle of rebellion of God's people, is that this cycle also puts the marvelous patience of God on display. God is indeed the great King of faithful and steadfast love. Of boundless mercy. A King who remembers the people of His covenant. A King who remembers us.

Talking to God:

This is not just 'their' cycle. It is the human condition. Our rebellion does indeed kindle the wrath of God. But His wrath has been turned away in Jesus. God has relented because He, Himself, stood in the breach for us. Because of His deep love for us, God sent His Son, Jesus, to intercede on our behalf. To bear the wrath we deserve.

If your response to Psalm 106 was like mine, you prayed prayers of penitence through every single section. As your sin was revealed to be like the sins of those who've gone before, you came to God with a heart of repentance. Friends, true repentance ends in praise because of the enduring love and mercy of God. As you end today, end with the Hallelujah and give praise to our faithful God with the concluding words of Psalm 106:

Save us, O LORD our God, and gather us from among the nations, that we may give thanks to your holy name, and glory in your praise. Blessed be the LORD, the God of Israel, from everlasting to everlasting!

And let all the people say, "Amen!"

Praise the LORD!

Day Three: Let the Redeemed of the LORD Say So! (Psalm107)

Though I've been married for twenty years now, I still don't feel qualified to give marriage advice. The success of our marriage – in that we are still together and for the most part enjoy each other's company – is mostly due to years of stumbling, falling, helping each other back up, only to stagger along together some more. If that isn't just a wonderful picture of wedded bliss . . .

I write what I do with a bit of humour, but also truth. Growing our relationship has been hard work. It is not glamourous, and the results aren't as quick or complete as sit-coms about marriage would lead you to believe. And sometimes, just when you think things are going well in the present, an issue from the past rears its ugly head.

One of the hardest lessons we learn in long-term relationships, and this is true of more than just marriages, is how to use past experience constructively in the present.

In a perfect world, when a present situation brings up past hurts or wrongs, we respond something along the lines of, 'Here is the lesson we learned last time. Thank you for being gracious enough to learn it alongside me again.'

Unfortunately, rather than being thankful for a willingness to kindly 'teach each other' lessons over and over again, we are more prone to bring up the past either like evidence in a courtroom trial where someone is going to be declared guilty, or to pretend it never happened and run from it like amnesiacs.

I absolutely love Psalm 107 because it is a teaching psalm. It models how to look back and learn.

In our journey through the Psalms, we have arrived at the fifth and final book of the collection. Book Three was characterised by psalms of increasing angst as the question of God's trustworthiness and His remembrance reached a critical point. Book Four was a resounding declaration that God is King on the throne. He does remember and He will act in remembrance of His covenant of love and mercy.

Book Five is an escalation of praise for God the King. However, in its many bold and boisterous calls to praise, it acknowledges the past. It does not start by running away from it. Yet, it also doesn't dredge up the past with a spirit of condemnation or a refrain of "See, you never learn?!"

Psalm 107 declares right out of the gates, "Let the redeemed of the LORD say so!" The redeemed of the Lord are redeemed because they needed to be. They got themselves into trouble and needed God to get them out. He did. This is a cause for high praise and thanksgiving.

As we turn to our psalm today, we are going to see different groups of God's people in four different situations of trouble. Four different accounts but all with the same result. People who were in trouble called out to God the King, who then redeemed, rescued, and gathered His people.

1. Begin by reading Psalm 107:1-3: Note the two reasons for which the psalmist encourages readers to give thanks.

2. Situation #1: Psalm 107:4-9 is the first account of trouble that some of God's people got themselves into.
    a. What was the people's condition in verses 4-5?

    b. What was their response in verse 6?

    c. How did God respond in verse 7?

    d. What declaration of praise is given in verses 8-9?

I know this is a bit of a spoiler, but I really want you to watch for this. This same pattern is going to play out in the three remaining scenarios. The people of God will find themselves in a crisis and they will call out to Him. In each scenario, God, in His loving mercy, saves them. And each time the people respond with praise and thanksgiving. This was the story of God's people. Their testimony. And this is God's story. The story of His faithfulness, His trustworthiness, His love.

We can trust God in our crises. He hears our cries and responds in love.

3. How have you seen God's hand in a situation or crisis you've faced? How did you respond? How has this become part of your story or testimony?

For I know the plans I have for you, declares the LORD, plans for welfare and not for evil, to give you a future and a hope. Then you will call upon me and come and pray to me, and I will hear you. You will seek me and find me, when you seek me with all your heart. I will be found by you, declares the LORD, and I will restore your fortunes and gather you from all the nations and all the places where I have driven you, declares the LORD, and I will bring you back to the place from which I sent you into exile.

Jeremiah 29:11-14 ESV

4. Situation #2: Read Psalm 107:10-16. This is the second troubling situation the people found themselves in.
    a. According to verse 10, what was their situation?

b. What was the reason for it according to verse 11?

c. The reason of verse 11 brings about a loving response of God in verse 12. What is God's loving response? How is this an act of love? What does this reveal about God's character?

d. Did it achieve God's desired result? (verse 13)

e. How did God continue to respond according to verses 13b-14?

f. What is the declaration of praise in verses 15-16?

God does not promise us an easy life. In fact, Scripture says, "*In this world you will have trouble.*" *John 16:33*. But that's not where it ends. The passage goes on to say, "*But take heart, I have overcome the world.*"

We don't have to live chained to our mistakes or sinful behaviour. We don't have to live in fear of the troubles of this life. We just need to turn our eyes to the cross - to Jesus Christ. We are loved by Him, forgiven in Him, and redeemed through Him.

Remember my affliction and my wanderings, the wormwood and the gall!

My soul continually remembers it and is bowed down within me. But this I call to mind, and therefore I have hope:

The steadfast love of the LORD never ceases; his mercies never come to an end; they are new every morning; great is your faithfulness.

Lamentations 3:19-23 ESV

Due to the constraints of time, we won't look at the next two situations in much detail, but as you read through them, pay attention to the pattern we've seen repeat itself in the first two situations.

5. Situation #3: Read Psalm 107:17-22. This is the third account of a troubling situation among the people of God.

Come to me, all who labour and are heavy laden, and I will give you rest. Take my yoke upon you, and learn from me, for I am gentle and lowly in heart, and you will find rest for your souls. For my yoke is easy, and my burden is light. Matthew 11:28-30 ESV

6. <u>Situation #4:</u> Read Psalm 107:23-32. This is the situation of the fourth group of people in trouble.

   a. Do you have a story about a time God stilled a storm in your life?

   b. How has this experience increased your trust in God?

   c. How has it calmed some of your fears?

7. Read Psalm 107:33-43. These verses depict two reversals the Lord will accomplish. They use several different images to show us the picture. In your own words, what are they?

Fear not, you worm Jacob, you men of Israel! I am the one who helps you, declares the LORD; your Redeemer is the Holy One of Israel . . . you shall rejoice in the LORD; in the Holy One of Israel you shall glory.

When the poor and needy seek water, and there is none, and their tongue is parched with thirst, I the LORD will answer them; I the God of Israel will not forsake them. I will open rivers on the bare heights, and fountains in the midst of the valleys. I will make the wilderness a pool of water, and the dry land springs of water . . . that they may see and know, may consider and understand together, that the hand of the LORD has done this, the Holy One of Israel has created it.

Isaiah 41:14, 16b-18, 20 ESV

Psalm 107 repeatedly prompts its readers to remember: This is who your God is, this is what He has done, so proclaim it. He has redeemed you from trouble – declare it.

As the redeemed of Christ, we must not run from the sin of our past in forgetfulness. Instead we learn from it. We don't remember it to glorify it or recall gritty details for the sake of a good story or vicarious fun. No! We remember it for the glory of God! We remember it so we can recount that even then He was faithful!

As the redeemed of Christ, we need not live in fear that God will keep bringing up our sinful past so He can rub our noses in it, and use it as evidence against us, proof of our guilt. He has all the proof He needs. When we recall the ways we have fallen into trouble in the past, it is to recount the ways He has redeemed us from our trouble. It is all for His glory and our good.

And as we remember our past, we see how God has acted out the greatest reversal of all time in Jesus. Sinful rebels have been adopted as children. Those who were far from Him in thought, heart, and deed, were brought near to Him in Christ. Through the work of the greatest reversal of all - eternal victory though death on a cross - God brought us into His very own family and made us heirs together with Christ!

Let us see this and be glad!

Talking to God:

Spend some time considering all the ways God has answered your heart cries. Remember His faithfulness. Remember His love. Tell of His great works. And praise Him for all He has done.

We are wise to consider the steadfast love of the Lord, and to declare His great salvation!

Day Four: The Beginning of Wisdom (Psalm 111)

I attempted to write an acrostic poem in preparation for today's homework. I was inspired to try because the psalms we are looking at today and tomorrow are acrostic poems. They are sometimes called twin psalms because of how tightly connected their content is. After the opening hallelujahs, the first word of each line begins with the subsequent letter of the Hebrew alphabet. So, I thought if I could write an acrostic poem, perhaps for the word 'Psalm,' it might be inspiring as an example and valuable as a tool for reflecting on the process.

At this point, you might expect to see an acrostic poem insert. You won't. I really did try, but my efforts were spectacularly awful! I guess the only thing I can take from my attempt at the process is – it's hard! I don't know if you've ever tried to write an acrostic poem, but the enforced structure can make it hard to achieve flow. The lines tend to stand alone, more like separate and distinct thoughts. And every time I have to come up with a word that begins with a specific letter, my vocabulary is suddenly reduced to that of a grade school student.

Just so you know, Psalm 111/112 are not the only acrostic poems in the Psalms. Psalm 119, all 176 verses of it, are an acrostic poem. Each stanza represents a letter from the Hebrew alphabet, in sequence. And it's not just the stanza that begins with the letter, each verse in that stanza begins with the letter the stanza represents. After my attempt at an acrostic poem with the word 'Psalms,' my head hurts wondering how the psalmists pulled it off.

So why did the psalmists attempt it? Well, one of the reasons is that in using every letter of the alphabet, the psalmists were expressing the indescribable depth of their subject. They were saying, symbolically, that the only way to even attempt to speak of the deep things of God, is to exhaust human language.[19] From A to Z (or in the case of Hebrew, Alpha to Omega), God is there, in it and over it all.

Another reason for taking on the constraints of an acrostic poem is that it forced the writers to sit down and think. When words have to be chosen diligently, one is more careful in how they convey their message.

---

[19] C. Hassell Bullock, <u>Encountering the Book of Psalms: A Literary and Theological Introduction</u>; Baker Academic, 2001, page 59.

1. With only ten verses, Psalm 111 is much shorter than the psalms we've looked at this week. Read through the whole psalm. What do you think the theme of this psalm is and what evidence would you use to support your answer?

Okay, here is where I would love to sit down and discuss your reading of Psalm 111. I'd love to chat about themes and sub-themes; to discuss your ideas and your support for them. This desire leads me to a quick aside: Doing Bible study alone is way better than not at all. Doing Bible study with a group is better yet. God created us for community. Not necessarily because being in community is easier. It can be easier to do it alone. There's less chance of getting hurt and nothing to stop you from doing it your way. We were created for community because we are better for it. All that to say, enjoy your discussion. Share your ideas even when you are not confident with them, and listen to the ideas of others.

2. As you were completing question 1, did you notice that the word 'works' or maybe the synonym 'deeds' was repeated five times in ten verses? It was! What is the psalmist saying about the works of Yahweh? Look at the following verses and jot down how God's works are described.

    a. Verse 2

    b. Verse 3

    c. Verse 4

    d. Verse 6

    e. Verse 7 and 8 (one thought carried through)

    f. What connections do you notice between the descriptions of God's works?

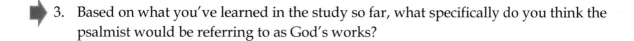 3. Based on what you've learned in the study so far, what specifically do you think the psalmist would be referring to as God's works?

We have looked at the magnificent work of God in creation in several psalms, but especially in Psalm 19. Two more psalms that declare the majesty of God's work in creation are Psalm 8 and Psalm 104.

Holy and Exalted God entering into covenant with rebellious humanity is another of the deeds of God that is extolled in the Psalms. He willingly bound Himself to people in a commitment of steadfast love, enduring faithfulness, and unlimited mercy. Over and over again the psalmists have appealed to God based on the promises He made to His people. Do you remember verse three of the 23rd Psalm? He leads us on right paths for the sake of His name. His name, Yahweh, is a promise! Psalm 105 is an example of another psalm that recounts the wonder of God's covenant with His people.

God initiated the covenant so He will act to protect the people of the covenant. He will defend and deliver them. He will punish them when necessary, for their own good and to draw them back to Himself.

These acts of God on behalf of His people are mind-blowing. Nature doesn't stand in His way – He is the author of it so has full authority over it. If a sea needs parting so His people can make their way through it, the sea will part. If His people are hungry or thirsty in a place where there is no provision, He is the provision. He will feed them with bread from heaven and water from a rock. Remember Psalm 107 and the four accounts of God's deliverance and provision for His people? If you want to read a psalm that holds high the character of God and exalts the ways He has acted on behalf of His people, go to Psalm 103, you won't be disappointed!

And then there is the work of God revealed to us in His law. (Psalm 119 - a very long acrostic poem - is a love song for the law!) God revealed the way to be in relationship with Him. He put a system in place that built a bridge – a bridge that stood in the gap between sinful man and Holy God. We are often tempted to think that the law is limited to the ten commandments we read about in Exodus 20 - the list of instructions that guide God's people to moral living. But the rest of Exodus is the law, too. There are laws about ceremony, sacrifice, and building a tabernacle – a place for God's presence to dwell among His people. These laws are not just to keep people busy and God entertained. It's the ceremonial system God put in place to reveal His character. It includes a system of sacrifice to show people that when the laws regarding moral living are not kept, God made a way to deal with that, too. The legal and ceremonial system reveals to us the justice of God. He won't overlook sin, but He provides a way for it to be covered.

These are the works of God that cause our psalmist today to begin with hallelujah! Praise Yahweh! This is what inspires the psalmist to give thanks in public displays of praise and gratitude.

4. In the second line of verse one, how is the psalmist giving thanks?

    a. What would the alternative be?

   b.   What is our theme for this week and how do you see a connection between the theme and this verse?

If we truly believe God is King it will impact our thoughts, our desires, our actions. Knowing that a sovereign, all-powerful King sits upon the throne of the universe and rules in justice upholding righteousness requires a response.

   5.   What response do you see in verse 2b?

   6.   What response is implied in verse 4a?

Let this be recorded for a generation to come, so that a people yet to be created may praise the LORD: that He looked down from His holy height; from heaven the LORD looked at the earth, to hear the groans of the prisoners, to set free those who were doomed to die, that they may declare in Zion the name of the LORD, and in Jerusalem His praise, when peoples gather together, and kingdoms, to worship the LORD.

Psalm 102:18-22 ESV

   7.   Turn to Psalm 78 (in the ESV, if you're using a different version). What is the title of this psalm?

       a.   What is the commitment made in verse 4 of Psalm 78?

       b.   Read verses 5-8: Why is the psalmist making this commitment?

Oh friends, if the works of God are our delight, we will study them. We will want to know them. We will want to share them with others.

   8.   What works of God in your life ignite whole-hearted praise and gratitude within you?

   9.   How does this passion translate into action? How are you making His works known?

The fear of the LORD is the beginning of wisdom; all those who practice it have a good understanding. His praise endures forever.

Psalm 111:10 ESV

Knowledge of the works of God leads us to knowledge of the character of God. We want to know HIM! And most of all, knowledge of Him will change how we live. We will live practicing the fear of the Lord. We will live practicing the way that leads to understanding. We will live by prioritizing that which will endure forever. And we will live proclaiming the works of His hands.

In the book of Revelation, the curtain is pulled back for us, revealing glimpses of how the redemption story which we are a part of will end. At the beginning of Revelation 15, an angel shows John a great and amazing sign in heaven which finishes the wrath of God. And then John sees what looks like a sea of glass mingled with fire. Standing beside this sea, holding harps of God in their hands, are those who have overcome. This is what John heard them singing:

"Great and amazing are your deeds, O Lord God the Almighty! Just and true are your ways, O King of the nations! Who will not fear, O Lord, and glorify your name? For you alone are holy. All nations will come and worship you, for your righteous acts have been revealed."

Revelation 15:3-4 ESV

Talking to God:

The exclamations of praise and thanksgiving that opened our psalm today will continue throughout eternity. When the people God has redeemed see with unveiled eyes the fullness of His works throughout history, they will not be able to stop praising God for what He has done.

Lift up a song of thankful praise; God has sent redemption to His people!

Day Five: The Righteous Will Never Be Moved! (Psalm 112)

Today we come to Psalm 112, the second of the Twin Psalms. Yesterday we looked at the big picture. We saw the works of God for His people as a whole. We spent time in the realm of theology - the knowledge of God.

Today the focus zooms in tighter. If yesterday was about God, today is about how knowledge of God impacts us. Yesterday's psalm said that those who have a right fear of God, not quaking terror but reverent love, will delight in God's ways, so they will study them and practice them. Today's psalm says once you've got your theology right, put it into practice.

1. Start by reading through all of Psalm 112. Now we are going to spend a bit of time comparing Psalm 112 and Psalm 111. As you look at the companion verses below, note the overlap.
    a. Psalm 112:1 and Psalm 111:2

b. Psalm 112:3 and Psalm 111:3

c. Psalm 112:4 and Psalm 111:4

d. Psalm 112:5 and Psalm 111:7

 e. Despite the similarities, what is different in every case?

This is the heart of what we've been looking at all week.

The image of the King should be reflected among His people.

His divine power has granted to us all things that pertain to life and godliness, through the knowledge of Him who called us to His own glory and excellence, by which he has granted to us His precious and very great promises, so that through them you may become partakers of the divine nature, having escaped from the corruption that is in the world because of sinful desire.

2 Peter 1:2-4 ESV

2. According to the verses above, what have we been given?

    a. How is it given to us?

    b. For what purpose is it given to us?

    c. What should be the result of us having received it?

For this very reason, make every effort to supplement your faith with virtue, and virtue with knowledge, and knowledge with self-control, and self-control with steadfastness, and steadfastness with godliness, and godliness with brotherly affection, and brotherly affection with love. For if these qualities are yours and are increasing, they keep you from being ineffective or unfruitful in the knowledge of our Lord Jesus Christ. 2 Peter 1:5-8 ESV

3. Peter begins the passage of Scripture above by saying, "For this very reason . . ." For what very reason? (Hint, look at what came before it.)

    a. For this very reason, what? What list of actions should increase in our lives?

b. What will be the result of increasing these actions?

Psalm 112, like Psalm 1, is of the wisdom genre. Remember, the wisdom genre is categorized by representing two ways to live. It showcases two types of people who have two distinctly different destinies.

Those of us who have chosen to follow the path of righteousness should find that it is a path of joy and delight and that it is a path that bears fruit. And the fruit hanging off of our trees of righteousness are not just for us to pick and eat. They are meant to be shared.

4. Where in Psalm 112 do you see evidence to support the ideas of fruitfulness and sharing?

One way to better understand a passage of Scripture is to check out other places it is used in the Bible. Psalm 112:9 is quoted by Paul in 2 Corinthians 9. Paul quotes this verse within the context of sending fellow workers to the church in Corinth to collect an offering they had promised for the suffering Christians in Jerusalem. Paul is telling the Corinthian Christians, Hey, I've been bragging about your generosity to other churches. Now it's time to make good on your promise. Don't make my bragging come up empty.

Paul reminds them that they were not obligated to give. They wanted to. And because they're not under obligation, they can give whatever they've decided in their own hearts to give – no pressure. But he also reminds them that God loves a cheerful giver.

 5. Why do you think God loves a cheerful giver? What does the attitude behind the giving say about the giver?

6. Turn to 2 Corinthians 9:8. As you read this verse, write down the word that is most repeated in it. (Depending on the translation you're using, also keep your eyes peeled for synonyms.)

 7. Read 2 Corinthians 9:8-10: What is the commitment of the One who loves generosity?

We can be generous people because we have a generous God. He doesn't give us a bit of this and a bit of that. He makes *all* grace *abound*, so we have *all* sufficiency, in *all* things, at *all* times, so that we can *abound* in *every* good work. I'd say that's pretty comprehensive.

We can freely give of our time and our resources because we know who owns them all, and we trust Him. We can be generous with our grace, our love, and our forgiveness, because we know who these qualities flow from and that He shares freely with all.

The righteous person of Psalm 112 has their theology right. They know who God is and therefore know He can be trusted to act. And they live as if they believe that this is true. They don't live in blissful ignorance that bad news isn't coming for them. They live knowing that when it comes, they are established by the One who can deliver them from it or sustain them in it. They know that their King will have the last word.

Do not fear what they fear, nor be in dread. But the LORD of hosts, Him you shall honour as holy. Let Him be your fear, and let Him be your dread.

Isaiah 8:12b-13 ESV

The righteous fear God, so they have nothing else to fear.

Friends, I think if I had to sum up the message of the Psalms, that might be it. It goes right back to Psalm 1 & 2. There are two ways. The way of the righteous and the way of the wicked. The way of the righteous will endure and bear fruit. The way of the wicked will perish along with even the remembrance of it. And when we know that this is what Scripture declares but our eyes do not see it to be true, we can know that the King is on the throne. Though opposition rages against Him now, one day it will be silenced. One day it will be permanently subdued and there won't even be any weapons left to fight with. The King is on His throne and there is no refuge from Him. But there is sweet refuge in Him.

And when we, His loyal subjects, live as if we believe this to be true, then delight, confidence, steadfastness, and generosity can be the hallmark of our lives!

Praise the Lord!

Talking to God:

Pour out your heart to your Father today. Ask Him to mold you and shape you into the image of His Son. To conform your desires with His. And to increase your delight in Him and His ways.

In the Sermon on the Mount, Jesus showed us that the way to blessing is through poverty of spirit, mourning over sin, submission of our wills to His, and an insatiable appetite for right living. Jesus said that subjects of the King will begin to look like the King. They will be merciful because they've received His great mercy. They will practice purity, because they desire to imitate the purity of their Father. They will be people sowing seeds of peace because their King has made permanent peace with sinful insurrectionists. And, Jesus tells us that living this way will bring the blessing of persecution. That part is hard. And doesn't really feel like a blessing. But it is. It refines and refocuses. It purifies and strengthens. And it leads to the great reward of heaven because the King will have the last word.

CALL TO PRAYER

Yes, they knew God, but they wouldn't worship him as God or even give him thanks. And they began to think up foolish ideas of what God was like. As a result, their minds became dark and confused. Claiming to be wise, they instead became utter fools.
Romans 1:21, 22 NLT

They 'knew' God, but wouldn't worship Him. They wouldn't treat Him like God or give Him the honour due Him, and they wouldn't EVEN give Him thanks. They knew He was Creator and even then wouldn't offer their thanks. They began to make up their own ideas of who God was, trading truths for their own 'realities' and the outcome was dark and confused thinking - without hope, without light. They assumed their enlightenment, but really, were nothing more than fools.

I'd encourage you to read the rest of the chapter in multiple versions and paraphrases. As I read, I certainly felt that the passage was speaking directly into current culture. And to think that the beginning of all this fractured living begins with knowing... but. The refusal to treat God like God. The refusal to thank Him. This leads to darkness and confusion, and to classification as a fool.

I looked up 'fool' in the Merriam-Webster Thesaurus. I'd encourage you to do the same. The images brought to mind regarding the word fool were specific and extremely unappealing. Some synonyms were even quite harsh: laughingstock, bubblehead, fruitcake, doofus, idiot, imbecile, stupid (to name a few). Antonyms included, but were not limited to: intelligent, sensible, logical, rational, reasonable.

If I want to live a life of wisdom and enlightenment, I must first acknowledge who God is and recognize that if He is all that He has revealed Himself to be (Creator and King, Author and Judge), a response from me is required. As we learned in this week's homework, our response should include a commitment to worship, a commitment to leading a blameless life, a turning away from the admiration of sin, faithless perspectives, and prideful responses. A life of wisdom includes fixing our eyes on Christ, rejoicing in His faithfulness, and delighting in His ways. Those who are wise seek to be fed and nourished by Christ alone.

We find an example of this kind of living in the life of David. He was by no means perfect and yet, in him we see a man after God's own heart. In this broken and sinful man, we see God's grace, love, and redemption played out. We see God's compassion and the power of His healing hand. We dig into David's life and into his failings - not to celebrate his sin or even to say that his sin didn't matter, but rather to learn from his repentant heart and celebrate God's redemption in bringing wholeness to our brokenness, and joy to our darkness.

In this week's homework, we looked at the cycle of our broken-heart problem. It begins with forgetting God and choosing to go our own way, which inevitably results in our cries for rescuing. God responds by rescuing and we rejoice and praise. Then we stop remembering to turn our attention to Him. We stop worshiping, so we forget and cycle again. How do we remove ourselves from the cycle? How do we fix our heart problem?

Practice

Praise the Lord! He has given us a solution for our heart problem.

Christ arrives right on time to make this happen. He didn't, and doesn't, wait for us to get ready. He presented himself for this sacrificial death when we were far too weak and rebellious to do anything to get ourselves ready. And even if we hadn't been so weak, we wouldn't have known what to do anyway... But God put his love on the line for us by offering his Son in sacrificial death while we were of no use whatever to him.
Romans 5:6-8 MSG

God made him who had no sin to be sin for us, so that in him we might become the righteousness of God.
2 Corinthians 5:21 NIV

If we are in Christ, Dear Friend, we no longer have a broken heart problem (as the enemy would like us to believe); healing is ours in Him!

Therefore if anyone is in Christ [that is, grafted in, joined to Him by faith in Him as Saviour], he is a new creature [reborn and renewed by the Holy Spirit]; the old things [the previous moral and spiritual condition] have passed away. Behold, new things have come [because spiritual awakening brings a new life].
2 Corinthians 5:17 AMP

... regarding your previous way of life, you put off your old self [completely discard your former nature], which is being corrupted through deceitful desires, and be continually renewed in the spirit of your mind [having a fresh, untarnished mental and spiritual attitude], and put on the new self [the regenerated and renewed nature], created in God's image, [godlike] in the righteousness and holiness of the truth [living in a way that expresses to God your gratitude for your salvation].
Ephesians 4:22-24 AMP

I wonder if much of our forgetting has to do with not being proactive. In order to not forget who we are in Christ and who God is, we must actively be remembering. Remembering what we are apart from God – dead. Remembering that in Him we've been given life. Remembering that every good and perfect gift is from Him, and all that we have is from Him and for Him. And this remembering should ignite thanksgiving and praise.

In the morning when we get dressed, we actively turn our attention to what we will put on for the day. (Young moms, I know that sometimes you actually aren't turning your attention to this, but are just throwing on whatever might be clean or even whatever might just be near. Blessings on you. This season will pass). What we choose to wear depends partly on what activities we will be participating in. I wonder how our days might be transformed if we similarly turned our attention to putting on our new selves just like we were putting on a new set of clothes. A new set of clothes can make us feel so lovely. And friends, there isn't anything lovelier than the clothes of Christ.

Put on your new nature, and be renewed as you learn to know your Creator and become like him... you must clothe yourselves with tenderhearted mercy, kindness, humility, gentleness, and patience. Make allowance for each other's faults and forgive anyone who offends you. Remember the Lord forgave you... Above all, clothe yourselves with love which binds us all together in perfect harmony... you are called to live in peace. And always be thankful.
Colossians 3: 10-15 NLT

You should clothe yourselves instead with the beauty that comes from within, the unfading beauty of a gentle and quiet spirit, which is so precious to God.
1 Peter 3:4 NLT

And all who have been united with Christ in baptism have put on Christ, like putting on new clothes.
Galatians 3:27 NLT

Because we have the nature of Christ within us by the indwelling of His Spirit when we received new life in Him, we are able to take on His character and values, thereby living lives of integrity and wholeness. Praise Jesus! Remember and thank Him!

On Our Knees

Acknowledge before God who He is - Creator and King. Worship, adore, praise, and thank Him for who He is and all that He has done and is doing. Thank Him for giving us good gifts through and in Christ; for forgiveness and reconciliation, redemption and righteousness, healing and wholeness, peace and restoration, power and presence. Whatever He brings to your mind as you behold Him. He is so good! He will even remind us who He is and what He's done while we are turning our thoughts and hearts towards Him, not because He needs our adoration to feel satisfied, but so that we don't miss out on the blessing of recognizing Him.

Ask for the Spirit's help in remembering. Ask for his help in putting on your new self, the clothes of Christ - righteousness.

Always be joyful. Never stop praying. Be thankful in all circumstances, for this is God's will for you who belong to Christ Jesus.
1 Thessalonians 5:16-18 NLT

REJOICE
PRAY
THANK

AMEN

Psalm 115: Listening Guide

Not To Us . . .

1. If the glory is God's, it's up to Him to figure out _____ to accomplish the _____.

2. If we're going to _____ differently, we'll have to _____ differently.

3. _____ glory is at stake. _____ will fight to defend it!

4. God ➡ Moses: "I will make of _____ a nation greater and mightier than _____." (Numbers 14:11-12)

To Your Name Give Glory!

5. When we don't give God glory, it _____ the state of our hearts; who _____ it more than He does?

Where is Your God?

6. Exodus 20:4-6: Don't make for yourselves a _____ or any _____ of your God.

7. Is there a _____ in your hand? (Isaiah 44:9-20; Habakkuk 2:18-20)

View this teaching session at www.unshakenministries.com

Our God is in the Heavens, He Does All That Pleases Him

8. Do your gods _____? (Exodus 19:16-20, 20:18-19; Hebrews 1:1)

9. Do your gods _____ or _____? (Exodus 3:7)

10. Do your gods _____? (Exodus 29:18, 25, 41; Ephesians 5:2; Philippians 4:18)

11. What do the _____ of your gods do? (Psalm 95:7; Isaiah 49:16)

12. Why do your gods need _____? (Isaiah 52:7; Psalm 77:19)

Run to Him!

13. Trust in Him, _____ of the covenant. Trust in Him, _____ of the covenant. Trust in Him, _____ who have learned to fear Him. He is your help and your shield.

14. All who are _____ to the one true God can run to Him for _____.

He has remembered us.

He will bless us.

Praise the LORD!

View this teaching session at www.unshakenministries.com

Week Nine: The Benediction

The word 'benediction' comes from the Latin word, 'benedicere.' 'Bene' means 'well,' and 'dicere' means 'say.' To speak a benediction, then, is to speak words of wellness, or to bless. Throughout history, Christian services have traditionally ended with the benediction to acknowledge the blessing God had instructed the priests to speak over His people. Before leaving the place His glory dwelled, God wanted His people to hear His benediction.

We began our study in the Psalms by looking at what it means to be blessed. We have come full circle. As our time together in the Psalms comes to a close, let us hear the benediction.

---

a WORD to the wise

The LORD bless you and keep you;

the LORD make His face to shine upon

and be gracious to you;

the LORD lift up His countenance upon you

and give you peace.

Numbers 6:24-26 ESV

Day One: The LORD Keep You (Psalm 121)

My husband and I grew up in a community where a dialect of German was commonly spoken. Early in our marriage we moved away from the community and, since we no longer encountered the dialect in the course of daily life, we fell out of practice using it.

Until our children came along. For a while we could talk over their heads by spelling out key words, but when the oldest one learned to spell, the game was up. We needed a new method of communication.

That's when we discovered the benefit of knowing a language they did not. When we needed to discuss matters they were not to be privy to, we began to have conversations in broken Low German, because that's what years of living among the English had reduced us to.

On one of our family excursions, Rob and I were discussing whether we should allow one of our sons to purchase a certain object. Because we needed to present a position of solidarity to our son, we had to come to an agreement between ourselves without his input. So we spoke in Low German. In our conversation we used the Low German word for 'thing,' thinking nothing of it.

Until hysterical laughter erupted behind us. The Low German word for 'thing' sounds like an English word that would not be used in polite conversation. A word that would not slip by unnoticed with three boys within hearing range. We were left to address misconceptions with some rudimentary lessons in Low German.

When we are familiar with a language, we don't often think too deeply about the meaning of common words. I realized just how true this was when I decided to look up the definition of the word 'keep.' I wasn't going to at first because I thought, "Seriously Arlene, that's one word you could probably be confident in your ability to define and understand." But I went digging anyway. My, oh my!

1. As opening brain calisthenics (is this a word you're familiar with? ☺), try to use the word 'keep' in a phrase, paying attention to as many different meanings or nuances of the word as you can. (And try not to peek ahead at the flashy definition below – that's cheating!)

Keep

/kép/

Antonym: release

to watch over and defend; to take care of; to continue to maintain; to retain in one's possession or power; to stay or remain on or in, usually against opposition; to continue to have and hold as opposed to losing, parting with, or giving up; to provide sustenance of someone; to own or look after for pleasure or profit; to honour or fulfill a commitment or undertaking

As you read definitions for all the meanings and nuances of the word keep, don't you just get shivers up your spine when you realize that the benediction God told the priests to place upon His people began with the words, "*Yahweh bless you and keep you?!*"

We are always in search of the blessing. We are always wanting words of wellness spoken to us and over us. Let us become a people who know where to look to find them!

2. Turn to Psalm 121, our psalm for today. As you read through the psalm, what word do you notice is most often repeated? (in the ESV)

Psalm 121 is the second song in a series of fifteen (Psalm 120-134) songs that are called the Songs of Ascents. While we do not know when they were written, for what purpose they were written, or by whom some of them were written (some have an author listed, Psalm 121 does not), we do know that the purpose for which they were used was pilgrimage. These are the songs the faithful people would sing as they journeyed to Jerusalem to keep the feasts God had given them in the law.

3. How did David refer to himself when speaking to the LORD in Psalm 39:12?

a. What is the significance of David describing himself in this manner?

b. What are the implications of being a pilgrim or on a pilgrimage?

c. Do you view yourself as a pilgrim on earth or do you see this world as your home? Explain.

Have you ever heard the idiom, 'your home is your castle'? The statement is not one intended to reflect the size or grandeur of a home. It is meant to convey the fact that your home is your domain. You are the ultimate ruler over it and thus you are responsible for its maintenance and protection. In fact, this idiom is established in legal code. In 1628 Sir Edward Coke, in *The Institutes of the Laws of England* stated, "For a man's house is his castle, et domus sua cuique est tutissimum refugium [and each man's home is his safest refuge]."[20] It is for this reason that others do not have the right to enter your home without permission, and why law enforcement needs a search warrant before coming in. Even the government is restrained against unreasonable entry and seizure of your home.

Your home is to be your safest refuge.

For us to experience this fully, we need a right perspective of home. We need to understand Who we belong to and what He is preparing for those who love Him. It requires us to know where to turn for refuge in trouble and uncertainty. Who do we trust to keep us, watch us, and protect us?

4. What question is asked in Psalm 121:1?

[20] Phrases.org.uk

5. What is the declared answer of verse 2 and what is the reason given?

⇨ a. How do you think the Psalmist's declaration in verse 2b relates to his statement in verse 1a? Of what is he reminding himself?

⇨ b. How might the pilgrim journey contribute to an increased awareness of Creator God?

When I initially thought of myself as a sojourner without a home, I conjured up an image of me wandering around with a bag tied to the end of a stick mournfully singing the lines, "*This world is not my home, I'm just a passing through . . .*" But in the drama of imagining myself homeless, I missed the point.

It's not that this world is not *a* home, it's just not *my* home.

We dwell secure in the castle of the King! We are not homeless drifters, but kept women who live under the care and protection of God. He is the One who establishes our refuge because it is His; He made it, He owns it, He will keep it.

Now don't misunderstand. I am not an illegal squatter who needs to worry about being found and kicked out. I'm here by design and invitation.

I'm not an arrogant heiress who looks down her nose at those who would call this world home and comment on the better home waiting for me. I'm like a grateful tenant who is aware that her landlord's care and protection extends to all and any who come to Him.

As we journey on earth, we don't lift our eyes to anything around us. We don't mistakenly believe that the hills themselves are a refuge. No! The God who made them is our refuge! We also don't look to the hills as insurmountable symbols of danger and hardship. No! We look beyond them to the God who made them and know that He is King over even the mountains!

6. Read Psalm 121:3-4: What does the repetition between verses 3b and 4a emphasize?

7. Read Psalm 121:5-6: How do you think the significance of these verses changes for someone living in a Middle Eastern climate (as opposed to us in the frozen north)?

8. What do you think the sun and moon symbolize in verse 6? What is the message of the Psalmist here?

9. What shift do you notice between verses 1 and 2 and the rest of the psalm?

    a. In what ways does this psalm point to God as our guardian and watch-keeper? (Hint: What are the three 'will not' statements of verses 3 and 4?)

    b. In what ways is God a source of protection? (Hint: What are the two 'is' statements of verse 5 in the ESV?)

    c. In what ways is God our refuge? (Hint: What are the three 'will' statements of verses 7 & 8?)

10. Do you experience the peace of knowing God keeps you and protects you both now and forevermore? Do you live each day with this truth in mind? What would look different if you did?

The word 'life' at the end of verse seven is a word that does not just relate to your body and the drawing in of breath. It is a word that encompasses the whole living person.

11. Turn to the words of Jesus in Luke 21:16-19. What is the apparent contradiction in these verses?

    a. We can be sure that the words of our Lord are trustworthy and true. What is Jesus really saying?

    b. Turn to John 12:24-25. How do these words of Jesus clarify or expand your understanding?

Is this not a psalm of confidence for us as a group of travellers?!

The King of the castle keeps us not just in our present journey, but beyond it, throughout all of eternity, world without end.

He is our defender, our provider, our refuge. He will honour His commitment to us both now and forever more.

The LORD bless you and keep you . . .

What a benediction. We associate benedictions with endings. I have yet to hear a church service begin with a benediction, yet I rarely leave a church service that has not ended with one. While we journey, the ending can seem uncertain. Will we arrive? And even assuming we do, in what state will we arrive at our destination? The benediction of our Lord does not have an end. It begins from this time forth, and it will last into eternity.

After this I looked, and behold, a great multitude that no one could number, from every nation, from all tribes and peoples and languages, standing before the throne and before the Lamb, clothed in white robes, with palm branches in their hands, and crying out with a loud voice, "Salvation belongs to our God who sits on the throne, and to the Lamb!"

Then one of the elders addressed me, saying, "Who are these, clothed in white robes, and from where have they come?" I said to him, "Sir, you know." And he said to me, "These are the ones coming out of the great tribulation. They have washed their robes and made them white in the blood of the Lamb.

"Therefore they are before the throne of God, and serve him day and night in his temple; and he who sits on the throne will shelter them with his presence. They shall hunger no more, neither thirst anymore, the sun shall not strike them, nor any scorching heat. For the Lamb in the midst of the throne will be their shepherd, and he will guide them to springs of living water, and God will wipe away every tear from their eyes."

Revelation 7:9-10, 13-17 ESV

Talking to God:

O God, our help in ages past, our hope for years to come, Our shelter from the stormy blast, and our eternal home!

Under the shadow of Thy throne still may we dwell secure; Sufficient is Thine arm alone, and our defence is sure.

Before the hills in order stood, or earth received her frame, From everlasting Thou art God, to endless years the same.

A thousand ages in Thy sight are like an evening gone; Short as the watch that ends the night before the rising sun.

O God, our help in ages past our hope for years to come, Be Thou our guide while life shall last, and our eternal home!

Isaac Watts, 1674-1748

Day Two: The LORD Shine His Face Upon You (Psalm 127)

Before we come to our psalm today, let me tell you a tale of two cities. No, this isn't a re-telling of Charles Dickens' story of London and Paris. The tale begins with the city of Babel. It begins at a time when all the people of earth spoke one language. Meanings and nuances were not lost in translation.

The people of earth migrated from the East and found a plain in the land of Shinar that looked like a good place to settle and put down roots. They worked together. Collaboration led to increased knowledge and skill. They became rather impressed with themselves and eventually called a town meeting.

Let's build ourselves a city and a tower, they decided. *We are accomplished people, let's not settle for any building project*, they said. *Let's build a tower that has its top in the heavens.* So the people of Babel got really busy building themselves a brick and mortar city.

"Let us make a name for ourselves," was the ambition that drove them.

God came down to see what they were up to. God saw what they were doing without coming down, but the point needed to be made that they hadn't managed to reach Him. God was not impressed with what He saw. He knew this was only the beginning. He knew He needed to put a stop to their actions, so He confused their language. They could no longer understand each other and collaboration ended. God then scattered them over the face of the earth. *Their* building project ended.[21]

It was time for *God's* building project to begin.

Instead of starting His project with bricks, God started with a man named Abram. God told him to leave his home and family and begin a journey with an endpoint known only to God. He told Abram to pick up his stuff and start travelling. God would show him where he needed to go when he needed to go there. And if it wasn't enough that man could road-trip with God Himself, God gives Abram a benediction.

God said, *"Let Me make a name for you."*

God promises Abram that He will build him a name. God told Abram, a man with no children, that he would become Abraham, a man with a great name who would become father to a great nation. God told Abraham that through him all the families of earth would be blessed.

Abraham would feel the smile of heaven. The warmth of God's pleasure. In receiving the benediction, he would become a benediction - a blessing. This was no small blessing localized for a family or a nation or a specific period of time. When God builds, it's on a big scale.[22]

 1. Why do you think the tales of these two building projects are placed one after the other in the book of Genesis?

---

[21] Genesis 11
[22] Genesis 12

With this fresh in our minds, we come to our psalm today. Psalm 127 is another one of the Songs of Ascent. Another song sung by journeying pilgrims.

2. Read Psalm 12.

    a. Jot down in point form what you see as the theme of the psalm.

    b. We can speak of 'building a house' with two different nuances of meaning. What are they? How are they demonstrated in this song? (Hint: See 2 Samuel 7:11b-13)

For building projects to succeed, there are three components to consider. First of all, a project needs a plan - a vision and a purpose. Secondly, the one doing the building needs to know what resources they will need and if they have access to them. Finally, a project requires a labour force to move the vision to reality.

The success of a building project hinges on the success of each one of the three components. The failure of the project can come from mistakes in any one of these areas.

3. Where do you see the critical mistake of the people of Babel? How does that compare/contrast with the success of Abraham?

4. What is the action of Psalm 127:1a?

    a. What is the action of Psalm 127:1b?

    b. How are you kept busy protecting, or taking care of what you've built?

5. Read Psalm 127:2 carefully and try to write the verse in your own words.

    a. What is the error of the worker in this verse?

    b. What would the opposite of this be?

    c.   What balance does the final line of verse 2 allude to?

    d.   Which extreme, lazy detachment or doing it all yourself, do you tend to drift to? What motives do you think fuel your behaviour?

Yesterday we uncovered the beautiful assurance of Psalm 121: the castle belongs to the King and He will protect and defend it. It is His domain under His care. The people of Babel were really busy building because they wanted the project to be theirs. They wanted the credit to be theirs. God responded by signalling out Abraham as His special project. Abraham would be built up into a nation which would proclaim to the whole world that the credit was God's.

6.   Turn to Hebrews 11:8-10. What reason does this passage give for Abraham's obedience of faith when he was called to get up and go?

Babel failed for the same reason Abraham succeeded: vision.

7.   **Ponder:** Look back at your answers to 4a and 4b and take time to do a building inspection. Do your building and maintenance projects have a healthy vision at their core? Does your vision align with God's? Are you leaving room for God to work or are you 'taking over' and building in your own strength?

Building projects are hard work. It's easy to lose sight of the vision. We can fall prey to the danger where we are stretched out on the couch of God's castle with an icy cold glass of water in our hand, watching the building and maintenance of His kingdom with lazy detachment. Not my house, not my problem.

On the other hand, we can get ourselves all hyped up with the opposite extreme. We can stress out with "a blasphemous anxiety to do God's work for him."[23]

And [Jesus] said, "The kingdom of God is as if a man should scatter seed on the ground. He sleeps and rises night and day, and the seed sprouts and grows; he knows not how. The earth produces by itself, first the blade, then the ear, then the full grain in the ear. But when the grain is ripe, at once he puts in the sickle, because the harvest has come."

Mark 4:26-29 ESV

---

[23] Eugene H. Peterson, *A Long Obedience in the Same Direction* (repr., Downers Grove: InterVarsity, 2000), 109. As quoted in John Goldingay, *Baker Commentary on the Old Testament Wisdom and Psalms Volume 3* (Baker Academic, 2008), 506.

8. How do you see balance between the two extremes in the parable of Jesus written above?

Some building projects centre around physical objects. Some building projects centre around people - building communities, ministries, families.

9. If you are involved in a project that involves people, how does the material covered today apply?

Being a mother of four, I could not leave today without including a quote I came across in my reading.

And it is not untypical of God's gifts that first they are liabilities, or at least responsibilities, before they become obvious assets. The greater their promise, the more likely that these sons will be a handful before they are a quiverful.[24]

If you are a weary parent, may that quote give you a measure of encouragement.

10. As we prepare to close today, read the last line of verse 2 one more time.
   a. Who is doing the giving?

   b. What is being given?

   c. Who is it being given to?

We are sitting under the benediction in our final week together. In this fast-paced world of frenetic building, is there any warmer smile from heaven than that of promised rest? Not laziness. Not collapsed exhaustion. Not activity resulting in perceived pointlessness.

It is the rest of one in need of refreshing after a day of purposeful and fruitful labour.

If the LORD is not building our houses, our work is in vain. But when the LORD builds the house, you can be sure it will be a project that, though the seeds of it look small and the sprout of it be slow, it will one day produce a harvest.

[24] Derek Kidner, Kidner Classic Commentaries: Psalms 73-150 (InterVarsity Press, 1975), 478.

The LORD make His face to shine upon you . . .

Numbers 6:25 ESV

Come to me, all who labour and are heavy laden, and I will give you rest.

Matthew 11:28 ESV

Talking to God:

O Carpenter of Nazareth, builder of life divine,

Who shapest man to God's own law, Thyself the fair design,

Build us a tower of Christ-like height that we the land may view,

And see, like Thee, our now blest work our Father's work to do.

O Thou who dost the vision send, and givest each his task,

And with the task sufficient strength, "Show us Thy will," we ask;

"Give us a conscience bold and good, give us a purpose true,

That it may be our highest joy our Father's work to do!

Jay T. Stocking, 1870-1936

Day Three: The LORD Be Gracious to You (Psalm 138)
gra•cious

from Latin gratia

esteem, favour

I am a teacher by trade and just cannot help myself. When the opportunity for review presents itself, I get pretty excited. It's just so fun to look back and see how time engaged in the learning process of reading, studying, and questioning, bears fruit.

Encountering Psalm 138 in this last week of homework is such an opportunity and I cannot let it go.

1. Read through Psalm 138 once just for the sheer pleasure of it. (It is a magnificent psalm!) Read it through a second time, making point form notes of all the words, phrases, images, concepts, etc., that stand out to you because we have encountered them on our journey through the psalms.

Isn't Psalm 138 wonderful?! It is a song of thanks for God's constant care. This is not a half-hearted acknowledgment of God's presence in the psalmist's life; it is the loud exuberant declaration of a whole-hearted worshipper. It is praise to the God he trusts and knows. It is a psalm of confidence because God is listening.

2. **What would you do?** If you were in a situation where you had to choose between something that was familiar but you knew it was unpleasant, *or* something that was unfamiliar - you don't know if it will be pleasant or unpleasant – which would you choose and why?

Most people would choose the familiar situation even though they know it will be unpleasant. This is why we have the idiom, *'better the devil you know than the devil you don't.'*

People intuitively trust what they know.

3. Do you know God the way David did? Do you know His character, His will, and His love? What steps will you take to grow in your knowledge and understanding of Him in the coming weeks?

If you've been tracking with all nine weeks of this study, you had to suspect I was going to take you back to Exodus 33 & 34 one more time, right?! I know there has been a lot of references to that scene, but it's because it's so pivotal. Because the scene is familiar to us by now, you will know the context just by reading the excerpts below.

. . . please show me now your ways, that I may know you . . .

Exodus 33:13 ESV

The LORD descended in the cloud and stood with [Moses] there, and proclaimed the name of the LORD. The LORD passed before him and proclaimed, "The LORD, the LORD, a God merciful and gracious, slow to anger, and abounding in steadfast love and faithfulness,"

Exodus 34:5-6 ESV

4. This is what David has in mind as he pens the opening lines of Psalm 138. What is David's posture in giving thanks? (verse 2)

    a. What is he giving thanks for? (verse 2a)

    b. What two things does David declare God has exalted (held high) above all things? (verse 2b)

c. What is the connection between His Name and His Word?

We have seen repeatedly in this study that God's Name is His character. His character is His commitment.

God's Name IS His word. It is His commitment.

This is our confidence. David knows that God will hear him and answer because the very Name that he calls out to, Yahweh, is the promise of that. That is why David can declare that God makes his soul bold in strength and confidence. Not because David has done some prolonged navel gazing and found anything to inspire it in himself. David has bowed down before the presence of God, meditated on the character of God, and come to know in his soul that when God lifts high His Name and His Word, it is a cause for whole-hearted praise and thanksgiving. This is what strengthens David's soul.

. . . before the gods I sing your praise . . .

All the kings of the earth shall give you thanks, O LORD, for they have heard the words of your mouth, and they shall sing of the ways of the LORD, for great is the glory of the LORD.

Psalm 138:1b, 4-5 ESV

. . . on earth as it is in heaven . . .

Matthew 6:10 ESV

David is a whole-hearted worshipper. The thing about people who worship with their whole heart is that they tend to be loud. Not necessarily just in volume, though that is often the case, too, but loud in projection. They can't keep what they love to themselves.

5. Turn to Psalm 40, another psalm of David. What is he saying of himself in verses 9-10?

   a. What is he desiring of his readers in Psalm 40:16?

   b. How 'loud' are you and why do you think that is?

God lifts His Name and His Word high. We are to do the same. Because the plan was always that the whole world would hear of His glory.

David, the whole-hearted worshipper, has right knowledge of how high and lifted up his God is. But David also knows that doesn't mean his God is distant and aloof. His God is personal.

He knows that Covenant God does not lose the individual in the crowd. David knows that those who bow in humility before this God will feel the smile of His favour upon them.

6. The first six verses of Psalm 138 reveal to us David's heart condition and emotional state. Exuberant. Confident. What does the opening line of verse 7 reveal of his physical circumstances?

a. As you've journeyed through the Psalms, how have you responded to the encouragement to let your knowledge of God inform and guide your emotions?

b. Though difficult, have you noticed shifts in your thought processes and mental dialogue?

Do you know one of the reasons why I love the Psalms? Because they are the unadulterated truth. There are speakers and teachers out there who speak some pretty impressive ear candy. They tell us what we want to hear.

All you have to do is believe.

If you can dream it, you can do it.

Reach for the stars.

If self-help worked, the industry would be going out of business instead of booming. Because at least one of the inspiring mantras would actually work and, having achieved success, there would no longer be a need for people to buy anything else.

People don't stop buying self-help because they don't stop needing it.

In a chaotic, messed-up world, we really, really, want to believe there is an easy path to health, wealth, and happiness. Sometimes we even buy those empty promises for a time because we so desperately want them to be true. But any fool can see that life is not always easy. Anyone with a heart beating in their chest has felt it break. They have known pain and empty promises.

The Psalms are a loud shout that we are not people who have been given empty promises. We are people who have been given promises of substance. We are people who, *while* we walk in the midst of trouble, *know* that the One who *walks with us* through the valley *will preserve our lives*.

Lest you think that sentence above is an empty promise, turn to the last verse of Psalm 138.

7. What are the verbs (action words) in the first line of Psalm 138:8?

    a. What will the LORD do?

    b. For whom will He do it?

    c. Why will He do this? (verse 8b)

    d. How long does His work endure?

The words of Yahweh last as long as Yahweh. Forever. The commitment of Yahweh, lasts as long as He does. Forever. He will never forsake the work of His hands!

And I am sure of this, that He who began a good work in you will bring it to completion at the day of Jesus Christ.

Philippians 1:6 ESV

We sometimes hear talk of care from cradle to grave. This talk is meant to comfort us because it alludes to security through the course of our lives. What God offers is WAY better than cradle to grave.

Tomorrow we will be reading Psalm 139. I don't want to spoil it for you, but we need to see this today:

My frame was not hidden from you, when I was being made in secret, intricately woven in the depths of the earth. Your eyes saw my unformed substance; in your book were written, every one of them, the days that were formed for me, when as yet there was none of them.

Psalm 139:15-16 ESV

The constant care of God begins before you are even formed and reaches through the unfathomable realms of eternity. That is how long He will hold you in His hands and that is how long He will not let you go.

Is there any greater benediction than this? That Holy and Majestic God makes Himself known to us through HIS NAME AND HIS WORD?! Oh friends, shout the benediction for all to hear – the LORD has been gracious to us!

And the Word became flesh and dwelt among us, and we have seen his glory, glory as of the only Son from the Father, full of grace and truth . . . From His fullness we have all received, grace upon grace.

John 1:14, 16 ESV

Talking to God:

O Love that wilt not let me go, I rest my weary soul in Thee;

I give Thee back the life I owe, that in Thine ocean depths its flow,

may richer, fuller be.

O Light that followest all my way, I yield my flickering torch to Thee;

My heart restores its borrowed ray, that in Thy sunshine's blaze its day,

may brighter, fairer be.

O Joy that seekest me through pain, I cannot close my heart to Thee;

I trace the rainbow through the rain, and feel the promise is not vain,

that morn shall tearless be.

O Cross that liftest up my head, I dare not ask to fly from Thee;

I lay in dust life's glory dead, and from the ground there blossoms red,

life that shall endless be.

George Matheson, 1842-1906

Day Four: The LORD Lift Up His Face Upon You (Psalm 139)

All week long I have marvelled at the benediction God set upon His people. The benediction of being kept, of feeling the smile of His favour and the warmth of His grace. Today we read that God also wants to bless His people by lifting up His countenance upon them.

After reading that line, your shivers might have settled down a little. What does it really mean? I'll admit it, when I first started hearing the blessing many years ago, that part didn't really move me because I didn't understand what God was wishing me.

coun • te • nance

a person's face or facial expression; support

The blessing Yahweh instructed the priests to give His people is that they would be blessed by God taking notice of them. That His face would be turned to them in favour.

Is the face of Holy God truly turned toward us in favour? That is the question we ask as we come to our final psalm of study.

1. Read Psalm 139:1-6: Would you consider the tone of this stanza to be active or passive?

   a. Who is the one acting?

   b. Write out a point-form list of actions referenced in these six verses.

   c. If verses 1-5 are the actions of one party, what is the response of the other party in verse 6?

   d. What is your response to the statements of verses 1-5? Why do you think you respond that way?

The theme of this stanza can be summed up with one fancy word: Omniscience. God is omniscient, all-knowing. There is nothing outside the realm of God's knowledge and wisdom. Nothing. No thoughts, no actions, no attitudes. David says that God's knowledge surrounds him, it hems him in behind and before. Another way David's words can be translated is by saying that God's perfect knowledge binds him up.

The only way my babies would sleep as infants was to be hemmed in or bound up. Or a combination of the two. Before laying them down to sleep, I would bind them up in a swaddling blanket, wrapping their little arms in close to their bodies so that their flailing hands wouldn't wake them. I restricted them so they could sleep in peace.

I know much 'Mommy advice' out there contradicts this, but I couldn't help myself. The other way I got them to sleep was to hold them close and rock and sing them to sleep. They slept content with the pressure of my hand of protection upon them.

If I knew I couldn't hold them for the duration of their nap, I would wrap them up before I rocked them. When it came time to lay them down, being bound up reminded them of the security of my presence. This reminder kept them sleeping peacefully.

2. Turn to Isaiah 66:13 and write down the opening phrase of the verse (until the semi-colon).

   a. Turn to Zephaniah 3:17: What is God pictured as doing in this verse?

   b. How do you relate these verses to a baby being swaddled so that it can sleep peacefully?

     c.   Is God's act of hemming you in primarily a comfort or a discomfort, and why?

We can respond in one of two ways to the omniscience of God. We can run from it in fear, or run to it for security and protection.

3.   Read Psalm 139:7-12.
     a.   Where are some places David is metaphorically running to, to escape the presence of God?

     b.   What did he discover?

     c.   Who or what is the subject of this stanza?

When we were studying the acrostic poems of Psalm 111 & 112, we saw that by using opposite ends of a spectrum (A to Z), the psalmists were making the point that while much of life is on a continuum, God is in, around, above, and below it all. There is nothing that is not under His domain.

4.   In what instances do you see this poetic device used in this stanza of the psalm? (Hint for verse 9: where does the sun rise? The Mediterranean Sea was west of Israel, symbolically the furthest you could go.)

     a.   What two things is the hand of Yahweh doing in verse 10?

     b.   How does Psalm 23:4 reinforce this stanza?

The theme of this stanza can be summed up with the word "omnipresent." God is fully present everywhere and at all times. Human constraints - like life and death, geography and topography, light and dark - they don't exist for God.

One of my children is afraid of the dark. He needs a night light because he cannot see in the dark. This limitation frightens him. It weakens the trust he had in what he knew to be true when he could see. Our keeper does not sleep. The God who leads us has perfect vision in the darkness. There is no place we can be where the hand that holds us loses its power. Not even death.

But it gets even better! It's not just that God isn't limited by the dark or that He is aware in it.

God is active and working wonderful things, even - maybe even especially - in the dark and secret places.

5. Read Psalm 139:13-18.

   a. Who is doing the work in this stanza and who is doing the responding?

   b. Who is the subject?

   c. What level of intimacy is inferred in this process?

The theme of this stanza is summed up with a wonderful word: Omnipotence. By now you may have deduced that the prefix 'omni' means all. Potent means power. God has all power. Not only is there nothing beyond the realm of His knowledge and wisdom, not only is there no place or time or dimension that God is not in, He rules over all of it. He exercises absolute power in all of it.

Psalm 139 is a beautiful psalm of God. He is the subject of every single stanza and we are the object. Every single time. He acts. We respond.

Why do I make this point? Because this is a psalm we have often used to lift ourselves high. We are fearfully and wonderfully made. Indeed, we are. But God forgive us if we fix our eyes on the created rather than the Creator who is above all and to be forever praised!

Sometimes our self-centered natures want to throw us a little pity party. "It's all about Him, nothing's about me so what's the point?" That is the point! It's all about Him so we must respond.

There are necessary implications for us if all this is true about God.

One of the implications in Psalm 139 that we cannot escape is the sanctity of human life.

I might know where your mind just went. *She's going to bring up abortion. And if she brings us abortion, she'll have to bring up euthanasia, too.* Yes. Sort of. All life is sacred. Planned meticulously, created intentionally. All life is specifically intended with great love and for a purpose. This is true of life still growing in the secret places of the womb, and it is true of life that we may struggle to see the purpose in or for.

If you experienced even a moment of self-righteousness those 'big sins' are not on your list of transgressions, please stop. Stop because there are many ways we can take life.

There are many ways we deface and dishonour the sanctity of human life. We have diminished life with cruel words. We have spat on the sacred with judgement rather than compassion. We have not only looked upon the unborn as inconveniences; we have slapped that same label on many lives that require extra care and compassion - lives that redefine a society's narrow definition of worth and beauty.

It is a serious thing to live in a society of possible gods and goddesses, to remember that the dullest most uninteresting person you can talk to may one day be a creature which, if you saw it now, you would be strongly tempted to worship, or else a horror and a corruption such as you now meet, if at all, only in a nightmare.

All day long we are, in some degree helping each other to one or the other of these destinations. It is in the light of these overwhelming possibilities, it is with the awe and the circumspection proper to them, that we should conduct all of our dealings with one another, all friendships, all loves, all play, all politics. There are no ordinary people. You have never talked to a mere mortal. Nations, cultures, arts, civilizations – these are mortal, and their life is to ours as the life of a gnat. But it is immortals whom we joke with, work with, marry, snub, and exploit – immortal horrors or everlasting splendors.

C.S. Lewis, The Weight of Glory

6. How do both the words of Psalm 139 and the quote of C.S. Lewis impact your view of the people you will encounter?

7. Turn to Isaiah 43:1.
    a. What does the fact that the people are called 'redeemed' indicate?

    b. How is God defining the people in this verse?

We are all people in need of redemption. But we are not defined by our guilt.

God does not define us by our guilt but by the name He put on us. His.

8. Read John 3:16-18: What did the love of God cause Him to do on our behalf?

You know how I love words. I love them because they carry meaning and communicate truth. When I first looked at the word 'omnipotent,' I instinctively broke it into its two pieces. Omni meaning all, and potent meaning power. I had to look up the definition of potent because I felt like I was missing something. What I found stopped me dead in my tracks. There is more than one meaning for this word.

potent

formed of crutch-shaped pieces; (especially of a cross) having a straight bar across the end of each extremity

All the knowledge, wisdom, presence, and power of God is communicated to us in the cross.

In the cross of Jesus Christ, God travelled the extremities of human existence and experience and said even there, I am. I will bind you up and hem you in. I will give My own Son as the ransom.

His life in exchange for ours, Jesus went into the depths of Sheol and forever defeated darkness with light. There is nothing beyond His ability to redeem. At the cross, we can declare with assurance that the benediction of His favour is turned fully upon us.

Talking to God:

He has indeed searched us and known us. We are formed with great care and attention and can live securely in His favour as demonstrated to us by the cross.

This is a benediction worth sharing with a battered world that tends to see their value in comparison, as a commodity, rather than seeing their worth defined by the Creator who calls us His and who created us to reflect His glory.

Pray that God will reveal ways you can share His benediction with a hurting world.

Day Five: And Give You Peace (Psalm 139)

The day I sat down to write this final day of homework, it was about -20° Celsius. I needed a hot cup of coffee, a blanket, and the fireplace. With all three in place, I wrote happily for a time. Suddenly, I was very uncomfortable. Engrossed in my writing, I'd missed the point when I moved from shivering to comfortable, and ended up way past that point. I had landed firmly in *cool me down - now!* The fireplace was turned off. The coffee exchanged for a glass of ice water. The blanket tossed aside.

Shivering in the cold does not appeal to me, but neither does sweating in oppressive heat.

Yesterday we wrapped ourselves in the warm blanket of knowing God is intimately acquainted with every aspect of us. As we finish up Psalm 139 today, that blanket might start to feel a little warm.

1. Turn to Psalm 139 and start reading at the beginning of the Psalm.
    a. After having meditated on God, what does David say in verse 17?

    b. How does David describe God's thoughts in verse 17b and 18a?

2. Verses 19-22 are David's response to meditating on the thoughts of God.
    a. Whose enemies does David refer to in verse 20?

    b. Who has David pitted himself against in verses 21-22?

c. Why do you think there is such a sharp transition from verses 1-18, to verses 19-22? How does David's meditation on God's ways in verses 1-18 lead him to his response in verses 19-22?

Does it just feel like the heat was turned up a notch?

It is far too easy to fall in love with the warmth of Psalm 139:1-18 without even paying attention to the heat of what comes next. We can find several verses in those first eighteen that would look very pretty sitting against a background of flowers on our social media feeds. I've yet to see verses 19-22 used in this manner. Why is that?

It's because it feels good to be reminded that our God knows all about us and will never let us go, but we get a little warm at the reminder that this truth carries an implication for us.

3. What implication do you see in the knowledge that God is aware of everything, present everywhere, and powerful over all?

The challenge to the absolute supremacy of God is how will we respond. Will we submit to His authority? Will we commit to His ways? Will we oppose His enemies? Of all those questions, the last one may seem the easiest to answer. It gets our blood pumping. It sounds like it's an excuse to start some holy warfare. We can get ourselves pretty excited by convincing ourselves that our enemies are His, and rub our hands together in gleeful anticipation of a little judgment coming down.

4. If the direction of David's focus is outward in verses 19-22, what is the direction of his focus in verses 23-24?

David does not keep the lens looking outward. He turns it on himself. I wish it wasn't true and that my own life did not provide so much evidence to back this up, but what is out there is in here, too. The seeds of rebellion and enmity against God grow in my heart, just like they grow in yours.

5. What is the difference between Psalm 139:1 and Psalm 139:23? Why do you think the difference is there?

6. Read Hebrews 4:11-13.

    a. How do these verses correspond with what Psalm 139 says about God?

    b. How do they correspond to what Psalm 139 says about us?

Friends, the statement of verse 1 is true. He knows it all anyway, even without the invitation. Would it not seem wise to see ourselves the way He sees us? Would it not seem wise to allow Him to expose the worst of us so He can do His work?

The only way He can apply His perfect wisdom, presence, and power to what is in our hearts with the warmth of favour rather than the heat of judgment, is if we respond to His invitation of intimacy with one of our own.

Search me and know me. Try me and know my thoughts.

See if there is any grievous way in me.

Lead me in the way everlasting.

I would be remiss to leave you with the coziness of the first eighteen verses of Psalm 139 and ignore the warning that follows - the same warning we heard in our opening week together. There are only two ways: The way of the righteous and the way of the wicked. The way of intimacy or the way of enmity. The way that endures through eternity or the way that will be wiped out along with even the remembrance of it.

How is this a benediction of peace you ask?! Well, this is the very best part.

The sin around us is in us. But (and it's a very big one!) we can run to God with it! We can invite Him to expose it because we can trust who He is. His name is our promise based on His character of steadfast love, enduring mercy, and unending faithfulness.

Because He has kept us even against opposition, because the favour of His countenance is turned toward us, because of the unfathomable blessing of grace through the cross of Jesus Christ, we can *KNOW* that we are loved and accepted *in spite* of our sins. We can confess our sins with complete security, knowing they do not impact our standing before God when we stand before Him dressed in His righteousness. We can pray, 'search me and know me' urgently, but without fear or shame because Jesus bought our peace with God.

But now in Christ Jesus you who once were far off have been brought near by the blood of Christ. For He Himself is our peace.

Ephesians 2:13-14a ESV

Our only refuge from the Son is in the Son; but what a sweet refuge He is.

In his commentary on the Psalms, John Goldingay writes, "Instead of our reading them, they read us. The way we read this psalm reveals something to us about ourselves, and God and invites us to ask why we read it the way we do and to try the other reading."[25]

7. **Ponder:** How have you read Psalm 139 and how has it read you? Have you read of the intimacy of God with pleasure or panic? Do you marvel at His ways as David did? Can you pray the final two verses with the assurance and security of knowing that God does not expose to shame but to cover up? Do you desire this level of intimacy with our all-knowing, all-seeing, and all-powerful Creator God?

The promised blessing of Psalm 1 is delivered. We can receive the final benediction of shalom - peace, wholeness.

My prayer is that our time together in the Psalms has ended with God's Word open before you, and your heart opened before it.

The LORD bless you and keep you;

The LORD make His face to shine upon you and be gracious to you;

The LORD life up His countenance upon you and give you peace!

Talking to God:

Oh, the depth of the riches and wisdom and knowledge of God! How unsearchable are His judgments and how inscrutable His ways! For from Him and through Him and to Him are all things. To Him be glory forever.

Amen.

Romans 11:33 ESV

---

[25] Ibid.

To God be the glory great things He hath done, so loved He the world that He gave us His Son;

Who yielded His life an atonement for sin, and opened the life-gate that all may go in.

O perfect redemption the purchase of blood, to every believer the promise of God;

The vilest offender who truly believes, that moment from Jesus a pardon receives!

Great things He hath taught us, great things He hath done, and great our rejoicing through Jesus the Son;

But purer, and higher, and greater will be, our wonder, our transport when Jesus we see!

Praise the LORD! Praise the LORD!

Let the earth hear His voice!

Praise the LORD! Praise the LORD!

Let the people rejoice!

O come to the Father through Jesus the Son,

and give Him the glory great things He hath done!

Fanny J. Crosby, 1820-1915

Manufactured by Amazon.ca
Acheson, AB

13406040R00120